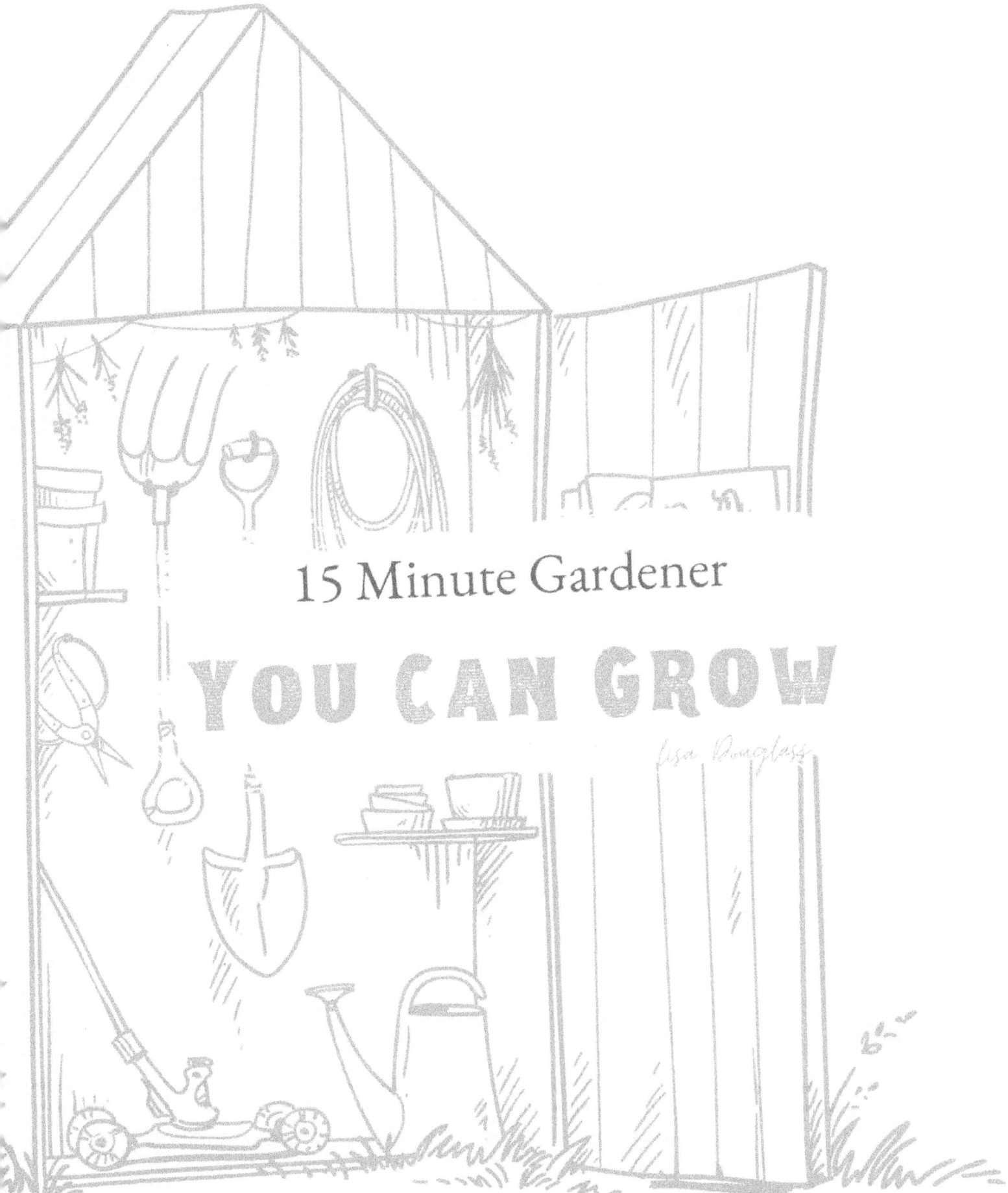

15 Minute Gardener

YOU CAN GROW

Lisa Douglass

DEEP RIVER GARDENS

First edition, April 2025

Author: Lisa Douglass

Graphic Design: Lisa Douglass

Select Drawings and Garden Plans: Sadie Douglass and Keira Douglass

Additional Imagery: Licensed through CanvaPro

Scripture References: Unless otherwise noted, all Bible verses are taken from the *New King James Version (NKJV)*.

This book is a work of nonfiction. Every effort has been made to ensure the accuracy of information at the time of publication. Gardening practices and conditions may vary depending on location, climate, and other factors. Printed in the United States of America For

more information, visit:

www.deeprivergardens.com

Instagram: @15mingardener

ISBN: 979-8-9919582-3-3

Dear Grandpa, Until Heaven…
Your love for family, food, and the perfect tomato changed everything.

For my children—
"When you see a bit of earth you want…. take it, child, and make it come alive."
—Frances Hodgson Burnett, The Secret Garden

"It is the glory of God to conceal a matter, But the glory of kings is to search out a matter."

Proverbs 25:2 NKJV

TABLE OF CONTENTS

TABLE OF CONTENTS

TABLE OF CONTENTS

Introduction: The Heart of a Gardener

Why Garden

New Perspective on Time

Do you ever feel like there is not enough time? That you run from one thing to the next without a pause? Life is a whirlwind; especially if you are juggling work, the care of family, and home, your time is stretched. So how do we maximize our time? The answer is in becoming purposeful with how we spend our moments.

What if I told you the minutes you're making important right now are seeding abundance you'll feast on long after the harvest? This book is not a rushed race to squeeze one more thing into an overwhelmed schedule—no. It's a quiet rebellion against the grind of this age. A decision to rest and connect. You may not be able to change everything, but you can change this moment. Taking 15 minutes a day to build a garden and a life that nourishes heart and home. And in the end, you'll realize that all these "15-minute moments"—well, they were everything.

This is a challenge in a culture that seems to reward those who hustle hardest. I get it. I have been gardening for 19 years, through 7 moves, 11 kids, 3 business start-ups, homeschooling and launching (my two oldest) and navigating three rather life-threatening ordeals. It's been busy. I get it. There have been seasons of frantic flourishing and seasons of dismal failure.

As a newlywed, three potted tomato plants graced my first apartment. I got something like one quart of tomatoes from those plants. But since it was more than I had ever gotten before I considered it a success. Success doesn't have to be huge to count. Small steps are so valuable.

Right from the start, I want you to know this is not a gimmick or trick. You can grow an abundance of vegetables in 15 minutes a day. I have stewarded garden spaces as a college student, working trick shifts in the hospital, as a new mom, pregnant, and as a new homeowner completely overwhelmed by the work of life. The hardest and most time-consuming part is figuring out what to do next. This book helps you maximize your time.

My first "real" garden was four raised beds that my father-in-law helped me build. At the time, I was getting ready for my final year of nursing school, eighteen months married and just a couple of months into being a new mom. Life was full.

Nothing in me wanted to give up more sleep, but everything in me wanted to grow...and a few quiet minutes. I still remember those deep breaths, running my hands over the plants I grew. It was a lifeline of hope. Don't get the wrong idea–I couldn't get more than 15 minutes of quiet on any given day. And there were MANY days I just didn't do anything in the garden. Motherhood is beautiful, precious, and *hard*.

But the garden grew. The garden taught me that consistent time and cultivated effort produced growth— yes, in my plants, but most precious of all was the transformation that happened in my own heart. In our little rented home, I had my backyard garden. The carrots and onions failed, but the tomatoes grew, and the lettuce was delicious. I had given what I had, and it was enough. I had a harvest.

Fast forward a couple of years, that rental home had to be sold, and we were left scrambling for a place to live. Thankfully, my parents let us stay with them while we searched for a new home.

Unfortunately, that painfully long process lasted almost ten months. It was another season of potted plants on the back porch. This time we got lots of tomatoes and herbs. I was growing. We were pregnant with Baby Number 4 when we made the radical life decision to move to the country. Happily, we signed the papers for our first real home—nine acres of woods that stretched us and our budget. I had tasted what was possible when we committed to growth.

The Heart of a Gardener

Fast forward to 2012, and I stood in front of a seemingly endless pile of dishes and cried. The weight of crushing responsibility closed in. We had our dream come true but, let's face it, we were not making ends meet. The stress of that and 4 children under 5 years old was immense.

I wiped my tears, left the dishes, and walked outside to the four mounds of soil I called a garden plot. Not one to sit around, I put in four raised beds. Only this time, I added a pallet-rimmed section for a potato patch and two more pallets marked an area for a play "mud kitchen" and sandbox for the kids to dig in. It was very messy. I scoured the library and researched everything about gardening. I decided to try what I call frameless raised beds. Something of a cross between what Charles Downing and what Gene in "Small Plot High Yield" gardening describes. First, you add cardboard, mulch, and six inches of compost to the top of the soil and create a garden. The cardboard attracts the worms that aerate the soil and the compost is a great nutritional boost to any topsoil. It was not fancy but it worked.

Back in the Garden

Back to that teary-eyed Mama in 2012, I walked out to the bushel of carrots my 4-year-old son had planted. We had never grown carrots successfully before. The interesting thing about carrots is that all that growth happens underground, and it is impossible to know what is happening until harvest. Sometimes you can have bushy greenery and then pull up disappointment. At that moment, I had to know. So I pulled at the abundant greens, fully expecting to find carrots that were failing as much as I *felt* I was in that moment. Giggling with delight, I called the kids – we harvested at least 20 gorgeous carrots from that bushel basket. I cried again, but this time tears of pure joy.

We grew so much food in 2012 on a shoestring budget. Most of all, I experienced the garden as a place of miracles. A place where I learned to nourish my heart and home.

The garden doesn't slow the schedule or make life more manageable. Those are choices we make. Time is still time and the garden can be just another chore. At the same time, choosing to grow can also help make all that we manage more beautiful.

The garden is where we were first made to come alive, and our hearts reverberate with that truth today. If you read Genesis in the Hebrew Bible, it begins with man and woman being placed in a garden. I believe God designed everything—from the science of soil to the mystery of pollination and genetic expression. The garden was meant to be a place of discovery.

When I think of myself as that teary young mom in front of a stack of never-ending dishes, I could not have imagined how a tiny decision to keep giving 15 minutes to God and the garden would change the trajectory of my life. You may not go on to dabble in farm markets, develop a passion for heirloom tomatoes, delve into soil health, or ever buy cows. But I hope you do dream and allow this 15-minute commitment to grow you in ways you didn't think possible. You are in the right space. You can grow.

That is My Why

The garden nourishes my heart and home and connects me to the rhythm of seasons and family. It gives my hands good work with substantial rewards. Most of all, I plant seeds because they connect me to my cornerstone: Faith. God becomes more real in the garden, repeatedly using my time there to reveal my own heart. So whether viewing the garden as a scientific wonder or an echo of our first purpose in Eden, one truth remains: growing food awakens something eternal in us.

Abundance blooms in the scraps of our time—just fifteen minutes a day. Plant one seed, pull one weed, and add a handful of compost. Each small action compounds, creating a garden that feeds both body and soul. The miracle of growth unfolds whether you can see under the surface or not. Your role? Show up, tend what you can, and trust the process.

Let's grow.

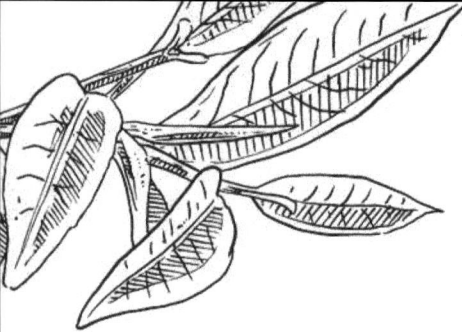

My Notes

"Working hard for something we don't care about is called stress; working hard for something we love is called passion."
– Simon Sinek

Part 1: You Can Grow

To plant a garden is to believe in tomorrow." – Audrey
Hepburn

How To Use This Book

So, how does 15 minutes a day actually work?

I love lists and action steps, so get ready for plenty of those in the coming chapters. Take it one step at a time, and don't give up. But first, let's look at what's ahead and how to use this book:

PART 1

You Can Grow— This is the meaty section that walks you through the main gardening phases: Prep Season, Plant Season, and Maintenance Season. This is where most of your action steps are taken so we keep things simple and super actionable. We also reference part three for various worksheets.

PART 2

Plant Families—A reference section where we go deep into plant families, growing instructions, and companion planting.

Keeping the Beet—This is all about the calendar. You'll find zone-based calendars, quick-start guides, succession plans, and more. Keep this section bookmarked because you'll come back to it often to stay on track.

PART 3

Garden Plans--- This is my favorite part. It's not an app. It's done-for-you, actionable plans with clear instructions and plant family guides so you can swap smart. No endless scrolling or overthinking—just plug and grow. When I first started gardening, this was what I wished I had, and I've spent the last 12 years making it a reality for you. These will work for any zone, just choose varieties that thrive in your climate.

On Repeat!

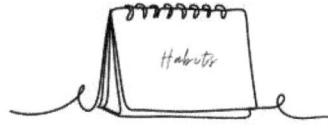

So, how does 15 minutes a day actually work?

I love lists and action steps, so get ready for plenty of those in the coming chapters. Take it one step at a time, and don't give up. But first, let's look at what's ahead and how to use this book:

THE WEEKLY BEET

Your "get'er done" rhythm. This is a fluid schedule that gives you an outline of how your typical week can go. When we are trying to optimize our minutes, decision fatigue slows us down more than actual work. The more we can "automate" by way of habits, the better. But don't worry—this doesn't mean you lose flexibility. Quite the opposite! If I've learned anything from nineteen years of toddlers (moment of silence, please), it's that nothing goes as planned AND predictability is a lifesaver. Schedules help you pick up where you left off when life inevitably goes sideways.

THYME CHECK

The teacher in me can't help it. I don't want to waste your time—it's too valuable. When a chapter has a lot of action steps, a Thyme Check is your reminder that this is a take-action book and is there to help you stay focused on the small steps toward success.

DEEP RIVER GIRLS' TEA

Before I show my age too much, I do love the slang use of "tea" (aka news/gossip). Only here, we're not spilling drama, but we are sharing fun facts, garden wisdom, and the kind of things we'd chat about over a cup of tea.

> "If you can fill the unforgiving minute
> With sixty seconds' worth of distance run,
> Yours is the Earth and everything that's in it…"
>
> —Rudyard Kippling "If"

Keep The Beet

CREATING REPLICABLE RHYTHMS FOR EVERY SEASON

The details will change with the season. Remember, the suggested tasks are not to be completed in one day. These are suggestions that you do based on the season and how easy or hard a task is to complete. Some watering may take no time if you have soaker hoses, so you may have more time to do something else on the list. Just fill the 15 minutes with the best of your time and attention. As you establish habits, you will find out what works best for you and personalize and make your own. I will say this—create the habit first. When life happens and you need to improvise, you can still "keep the beet".

MONDAY: MAINTAIN ON MONDAY—CULTIVATE, PLANT & BUG CHECK

This is a day to do the things that keep your garden running. Here are a few suggested maintenance activities:
- Cultivate: Run a finger hoe between plants to disturb weeds before they have a chance to get large. This is key. Large weeds = lots more time.
- Check for signs of pests.
- Plant seeds.
- Sharpening a tool, making a planting plan, or ordering seeds.

TUESDAY: TRIM ON TUESDAY—PRUNE, HARVEST & BUG CHECK

- Prune plants as needed (Refer to Solanaceae Family: Tomatoes and Cucumbers for tips).
- Trellis vining veggies.
- Bug check: bring a cup of soapy water and brush bugs and larvae into it. (Do this more often if you are struggling with infestation).

WEDNESDAY—WEED AND WATER

- Run a finger hoe gently around plants to disturb the soil and pull by hand any weeds that are big enough to be picked and removed.
- Water your plants if needed (drip or sprinkler). Use common sense: if it is raining or just rained you do not need to water.
- You can also add planting here in the spring.

Keep The Beet

THURSDAY—PEST & OTHER PROBLEMS

- Perform a detailed pest inspection. Do this check with a cup of soapy water to dispose of any unwanted creepy crawlies.
- **Identify new issues:** or problems and make a note in your journal about anything you have questions about.
- **Inspect Storage Areas:** Check stored items for literal bugs, like weevils, stink bugs, or any other creepy crawlies. If storing dahlia bulbs, peek at them.
- **Prepare for Solutions:** Review your garden journal, note any problems and research solutions.

FRIDAY—HAPPY HARVEST

- **Reflect:** Review your garden notes from the past season. What worked? What didn't?
- **Record:** Update your journal with insights and plans for the next season. Identify what crops you'd like to focus on next year.

SATURDAY—PLANT

- **Sow seed, transplant or pot up.**
- **Review Goals:** Look at your long-term gardening goals. Are there new skills you want to learn or crops you want to try? Make a note in your journal.
- **Reset:** Tidy your workspace or storage area. Sharpen and oil tools or repair trays and pots. In slower season remember that preparing is planting seeds for the future garden.

SUNDAY—REST

- Recharge: Take the day to rest and enjoy your garden, even if it's just imagining how it will look in spring.
- Reflect on how your systems and habits could grow. Plan improvements to make your gardening journey even more enjoyable and efficient.

- That's it. Those are the tasks. Everything can be done in 15 minutes every day. Gardens need consistency and when you deliver on that need everything flourishes. You can garden. Write on a sticky note. Set a reminder on your phone. You can do this!

SETTING THE PACE

The goal of the 15-minute method is to cut the learning curve and give you clear, actionable steps to accomplish more in less time. What are the first three game-changers? First, you'll commit to being in your garden for 15 minutes, six days a week. I fully support taking a rest day to just sit and enjoy time in your garden space.

Second, you will establish a weekly rhythm of work—think Laura Ingalls Wilder's "Wash on Wednesday." By doing this we create habits that reduce decision fatigue and put the garden on "auto-pilot." I call this system "The Weekly Beet" (see the end of this chapter). For example: when you have a habit of "Weeding on Wednesday," even during the winter you know what to do. "Weeding" might mean evaluating and removing things that do not support growth, such as broken tools, empty seed packets, or cracked garden trays. A task comes up and write it down to address on the appropriate day.

Lastly, start small. Ask any experienced gardener or open any gardening book, and you'll find the same warning: "Don't overplant." Gardening is exciting and addictive. But when your garden exceeds your time, budget, and abilities, it becomes a recipe for burnout.

I recommend starting with four 4x8 raised beds, 2ft high. Could you manage six in 15 minutes a day? Probably. Eight? Maybe. But it's the "probably" and "maybe" territory we're avoiding here. Expanding at a pace that matches your skill and time commitment makes it more likely you'll stick with it for the long haul.

Think of it like the "snowball strategy" for paying off debt. Dave Ramsey, the debt guru, advises tackling the smallest debt first and then rolling those payments into the next largest debt, building momentum and paying off debts faster. The same principle applies to gardening. Starting small helps you gain experience, improve your skills, and build efficiency. Before long, you'll accomplish things you once thought were impossible.

Why It Works

- Small gardens are easier to maintain. Starting with weed-free raised beds makes it simple to maintain.
- Planting and watering are routine tasks. Once you find your rhythm, tasks take no time at all. You'll naturally spend more time outdoors, flipping through garden catalogs, and enjoying life.

- You'll savor the harvest. Whether it's picking flowers for the kitchen table, slicing tomatoes for dinner, or simply admiring your garden, every little win is worth celebrating. The more you celebrate, the more momentum you'll gain!

Let's build a garden that nourishes both your home and your heart.

Task #1 Dream Big and Set a Time

Pick 15 minutes and commit to that time today. Try to make it in the morning because the garden is a morning person and needs that time before the pressure of heat to thrive.

Write your time here:_____

Whatever your season or garden size, I want you to feel so empowered by these small wins. The 15-minute method is about consistency, simplicity, and using minimalist strategies to cut through garden overwhelm. It's about creating sustainable rhythms that expand as your garden grows. The reason why your garden should feel like an extension of the values you use to build your home—imagine quiet spaces for rest, sharing stories while picking weeds, and making memories with every harvest.

For me, it's always been about family. I'll never forget our first big garden (3000 sq. ft.!) and the game of "Hot Lava," where my kids learned to keep their feet out of the beds by imagining molten lava beneath them. They collected "gold" from the soil-rocks, really-and turned weeding into treasure hunting. Those games turned work into play, and the garden became a place of laughter, storytelling, and connection. Even now, years later, I catch my kids smiling when I ask if they want to "treasure hunt."

Whether you make rocks "gold" or turn the garden beds into "hot lava", make it fun. Your garden is your canvas, and your "why" is the story you'll paint. Whether it's creating moments of joy with your family, achieving self-sufficiency, or simply finding time for yourself, dig in, dream big, and let the seeds you plant today grow into the life you envision tomorrow. Your "why" will carry you further than any strategy or method--because it's the heart of everything you do.

Task #2 Create a Sun Map for Your Garden

Observe Your Space

- Track sunlight at different times of the day (morning, midday, afternoon).
- Note shaded areas from trees, buildings, or fences.
- Observe how light shifts throughout the seasons.

Time-Based Sun Exposure

- Full Sun (6+ hours) - Best for tomatoes, peppers, squash, and melons.
- Partial Sun (4-6 hours) - Good for root crops, herbs, and some flowers.
- Partial Shade (2-4 hours) - Ideal for leafy greens, lettuce, and brassicas.
- Full Shade (Less than 2 hours) - Limited options, but can work for ferns or shade-tolerant edibles like mint.

Mapping Your Garden

- Sketch out your garden layout.
- Mark areas based on how much sun they receive.
- Use arrows to show the direction of sunlight movement.

Tools to Help

- Notebook & Pencil- Simple tracking throughout the day.
- Time-Lapse Camera -A set-it-and-forget-it option.
- Garden Apps -Some apps can help analyze sun exposure based on location

The Weekly Beet

Creating Rhythms for Every Season

One of the most powerful tools in the 15 Minute Gardener's toolbox isn't a shovel or a seed packet— it's rhythm. Establishing a weekly gardening routine puts your garden care on autopilot and dramatically reduces decision fatigue. When you know what to do each day, the time you spend in the garden becomes focused, efficient, and easy to repeat—season after season.

As you settle into this rhythm, the question shifts from "What should I do next?" to "What day is it?" That's the power of routine. With just 15 minutes a day, a simple weekly flow transforms scattered effort into steady, sustainable progress.

What follows is the framework I've used for years—a daily guide that keeps your garden moving forward, adapts with the seasons, and helps you stay grounded even when life gets busy.

Garden Thyme Checks

Keeping the 15-Minute Gardener Rhythm–
Remember—it's not a schedule it's a flow.

- **Define Your Why** - This helps you focus on you, your family, the environment you are creating. Otherwise, this adventure has the potential to be just another chore. (15 min)
- **List 3-5 specific goals** (such as: grow tomatoes, start compost, relax once a week in the garden space...)
- **Finish Prep Season** (Time varies)
- **Garden Site Assessment**
  - Walk the potential space and photograph at different times of day, note sunlight patterns, and make sure you are getting 8-12 hrs of sun. Note: Pick a day you'll be home and can peek out the window once every hour.
- **Create Your Garden Space**
  - First 15: Mark off your space with twine and stakes
  - Next 15: add one personal touch (think garden chime, birdhouse, painted rock. Keep it simple. Something that says, "This space is special".
  - Start Your Garden Journal (15 min) Write down what vegetables you love to eat. Use the checklist in the back.
  - Make sure to date your first entry.
- **Mini Skills Assessment** (15 min)
  - Identify three skills to develop
  - Write down your biggest gardening concerns
- **First Week Planning (15 min)**
  - Choose a consistent time
  - Set up your reminder system— Zone 5-6 can use the calendar in the back
- **Be Still and Know (15 min)** —Take 15 minutes to simply sit and savor this new beginning

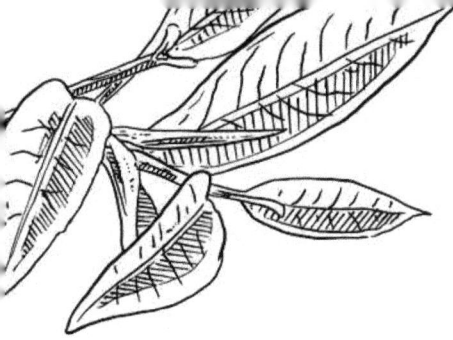

My Notes

This is not a rushed race to cram on more thing into a packed schedule.
A garden is a quiet rebellion against a world that pushes us to preform.

— Lisa

Prep Season

- Soil Science
- Garden Set Up
- Budget
- Grocery Calculator
- Pick a Place
- Seed List

No one is born with a green thumb.
Green thumbs are earned by showing up.

THE 15-MINUTE

Prep Season Checklist

Here's a look at what your Prep Season might look like depending on when you start. These are simple tasks that can be compressed into about a month before your last frost date. That said, you have time to spread these tasks out. Go for it!

If Prep season starts in the spring, your activities get squeezed into a shorter time frame. See *0=60 Get Growing* in the back for a 36-day quick start guide.

September - October

Research gardening basics (books, podcasts, videos) HINT: *Read this book.*

Plan garden layout. Do the quiz and use the plans in the back of the book!

Order garden supplies:

Raised bed materials

Soil

Collect cardboard and leaves

Source-free compost and manure

Begin composting or source quality soil

November - December

Create a seed list

Organize garden tools and supplies

Make a wish list of needed tools

Start a worm farm. (Not required, but so fun and practical)

January - February

Finalize garden layout and seed list. Get on these catalog lists: Botanical Interests, High Mountain Mowing, and True Leaf Market

Order seeds for the spring

Read about companion planting or specific plant care for your chosen varieties

Learning to Grow

In the Prep Season, the focus is on learning and building. These are the big-ticket tasks that will form the foundation you need to grow.

First, we learn! This chapter will cover the raised bed basics and why that is the garden you want to have. We'll cover the budget and give strategies for saving money and getting started, regardless of your bottom line.

If you find you have extra moments for study, get creative with your learning time. The most important task is to stay focused and read this book. If you need some audiovisual learning, we've got plenty of other resources on our website, *DeepRiverGardens.com,* and Instagram, *@15mingardener*—but remember, it's all about enjoying the process and this handbook was written so you would have everything you need for many seasons to come!

Get Ready to Build

Create a Plan: We can't build without a plan! In this chapter, we'll map out where you'll grow, decide on your crop list, and plot out your garden space.

Compile a Seed List. Finally, we look at "The Veggies You Eat." We'll make a list of seeds you'll need for the season, based on foods your family loves. The second focus is on direct sow. Starting seeds is tricky so for the first year we skip that and focus our efforts on what we can sow from seed or purchase and plant directly. Lastly, we have ready-made garden plans at the back of the book so you'll know exactly what to plant for all-season abundance.

Keeping the Minutes:
Some tasks, like shopping for supplies or setting up the garden, may take time upfront. Just remember to break these up into smaller chunks. To save time order supplies online and have them delivered or pick them up while running errands. Our tiny local hardware store has online ordering with pick-up at no cost. Take advantage of these. emember, you've got this! Next, let's figure out one o the most important aspects — our budget.

"Gardening is an instrument of grace." —May Sarton

Start With a Budget: Roots and Realities

While many will complain it's too expensive to garden-it's not if you garden smart. Recent studies show that:

- **$600 a Year in Savings:** The average household can save up to $600 a year by growing key crops like tomatoes, peppers, and leafy greens *(National Gardening Association, 2003)*.

- **Urban Agriculture Feeds the World:** Urban gardens contribute to 15-20% of the world's food supply, proving that even small spaces can make a significant difference *(FAQ Urban Agriculture Report, 2021)*.

- **Reducing Waste, One Leaf at a Time:** Gardens help cut food waste by encouraging you to harvest only what you need and compost what you don't *(NRDC Food Waste Report, 2017)*.

Here's a wild stat: nearly 40% of food in the U.S. goes to waste. Let that sink in for a moment. All that labor, fuel, and energy poured into growing food. 40% is completely wasted—it ends up uneaten and in landfills. It's upsetting, isn't it? But that's where your garden comes in. Every seed you plant is a step toward breaking that cycle. One tomato at a time, you're reconnecting with the process, reducing waste, and making a meaningful impact.

This isn't just about food—it's about showing up for something bigger. A garden, no matter how small, contributes to a more sustainable future. Plus, let's be honest: nothing beats the first crunch of carrots you grew yourself.

"Build houses and live in them; and plant gardens and eat their produce."--Jeremiah 23:5 NASB1995

Budget Breakdown - What You Need to Get Started

Step 1: Pick a Plan - What's Your Budget?

Even before you've found your perfect spot for the garden (we'll get to that in the next section), it's time to think about how much you're willing to spend. Starting a garden doesn't have to be expensive but it is best to put in a little upfront investment that can save you time and hassle later on.

If you can swing it, I recommend starting with the **$400 Plan**. It strikes a good balance between making a solid investment, getting decent raised bed durability—and staying frugal. Remember this is an initial investment. Your ongoing costs will mainly be for seeds (you can save many) and starter plants (you can grow into starting your own). Let's take a look at the budget breakdown based on your garden size and materials.

Get 'Er Done Budget Plan - $200

- **Seeds:** $50
- **Starter Plants:** $50
- **Garden Planner & Book:** $45
- **Tools/Trays:** $50
- **Free Soil** (We'll guide you through finding good local soil)

Pros: This plan gets you started quickly and cheaply! You'll likely have extra seeds for succession sowing and the setup is fast.

Cons: Free soil could be rocky, weedy, or chemical-laden, so be ready for a little extra TLC and keep in mind that you may have to spend more time maintaining the soil and weeding. It's really hard to stay in the 15-minute framework and hand-source free materials.

Investment Budget Plan - $400

- **4 Raised Beds (Metal from Amazon):** $170
- **Seeds:** $50
- **Starter Plants:** $75
- **Garden Planner & Book:** $45
- **Tools/Trays:** $50
- **Soil $200 + $30 in Seed Starter:** Top of the raised beds with high-quality soil

Pros: More durable and sustainable than the $200 plan. This is a long-term investment that saves time and effort.

Cons: Slightly higher upfront cost, but worth it for ease and longevity.

Beautiful Budget Plan - $1000+

- **4 Raised Beds {Metal/Wooden/Cedar}:** $200-400 each
- **Seeds:** $50

- **Starter Plants:** $75
- **Garden Planner & Book:** $45
- **Tools/Trays:** $50
- **Purchased Organic Compost:** $40/yard ($200 for 5 yards)
- **Mulch for Borders:** $200 (optional-you can mow around beds)

Pros: Stunning setup with long-lasting materials. Perfect for those who want both durability and a beautiful garden.

Cons: Higher initial cost, but the payoff is years of productivity and aesthetic appeal.

The budget for your garden is a big deal. Like any home project, realize that there will be unexpected costs and savings but rarely will your garden end up under budget. So give yourself some wiggle room. The budget will ultimately determine what you buy and how you set up your space. Remember this: Bigger is not better, and done is better than perfect.

Significant Other Sway Sheet

Do you have someone skeptical that the garden is going to pay off? We've included a "Significant Other Sway-Sheet" to break down exactly how your garden can easily yield triple on the investment. The facts are pretty persuasive.

ACTION STEP: Check out the next section for the Significant Other Sway-Sheet. This is not about arm-twisting. We walk through the real costs and time commitments. We want you to succeed and we believe we grow stronger together so even if your significant other doesn't garden, you can at least be agreed it is a good investment of time and money.

P.S. If you're asking your significant other for input on a big-ticket garden purchase, give them more than 15 minutes. Just sayin'.

Significant Other Sway-Sheet

Four Raised Beds

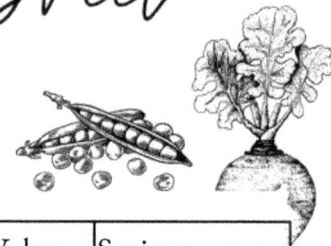

Vegetable	Row Ft	Spacing (in)	Seed	Price	Est. Harvest	Est. Value	Savings
Garlic	24	6	~¼ lb (35 cloves)	$7.50	35 bulbs	$35	$27.5
Onions	24	6	~1 oz	$2.99	24 lbs	$48	$45.31
Peas	24	2	~1 oz	$2.99	12 lbs	$36	$33.31
Radishes	24	2	~1 oz	$2.99	10 lbs	$20	$18.01
Swiss Chard	24	6	~1 oz	$2.99	15 lbs	$45	$42.31
Kale	24	12	~0.5 oz	$2.99	20 lbs	$60	$57.31
Beets	24	3	~2 oz	$2.99	20 lbs	$40	$37.31
Carrots	24	2	~1 oz	$2.99	20 lbs	$40	$37.31
Lettuce Mix	24	6	~0.5 oz	$2.99	15 lbs	$45	$42.31
Cucumbers	24	12	~1 oz	$2.99	30 fruits	$30	$27.31
Summer Squash	24	24	~0.5 oz	$2.99	40 fruits	$80	$77.31
Winter Squash	24	36	~0.5 oz	$2.99	20 fruits	$65	$62.31
Bush Beans	24	4	~4 oz	$2.99	15 lbs	$45	$42.31
Tomatoes	N/A	N/A	4 plants	$3.50 each	40 lbs	$80	$76.50
Peppers	N/A	N/A	6-pack	$3.49 per pack	10-20 per plant in fertile soil	$75	$71.50

Total Estimated Costs and Returns:

Total Seed Cost: Approximately $45

Total Transplant Cost: $3.50 × 4 (tomatoes) + $3.49 (peppers) = $17.49

Total Investment: $45 + $17.49 = $62.49

Total Estimated Harvest Value: Approximately $619

This plan gives you enough seed to cover a full season's worth of growth, with leftover seed for 1-2 future seasons. I would argue that the $619 figure is SUPER low but I would rather estimate conservatively. The bottom line is that your investment today will be paying off in both harvest and cash saved for tomorrow.

Significant Other Sway-Sheet

Growers Garden

Vegetable	Row Ft	Amount	Seed Price	Estimated Harvest	Estimated Value	Net Value
Garlic	100 ft	10 lbs (1/4 lb = 35 bulbs)	$60	400 bulbs	$400	$340
Onions (early greens)	100 ft	2 packets	$5.98	400-600 green onions	$150	$144.02
Leeks	100 ft	2 packets	$5.98			
Onions (cooking)	100 ft	2 packets	$5.98	200 onions	$100	$94.02
Sweet Onion	100 ft	2 packets	$5.98	100 onions	$100	$94.02
Radish (Red)	100 ft	2 packets	$5.98	200 radishes (3-4 harvests)	$60	$54.02
Swiss Chard	100 ft	4 packets	$11.96	Approx. 140 lbs	$140	$128.04
Kale	100 ft	4 packets (use for baby leaves)	$11.96	Approx. 140 lbs over 5 months	$150	$138.04
Bok Choy (Asian Spinach)	100 ft	1 packet	$2.99	40-60 lbs	$80	$77.01
Spinach	100 ft	4 packets	$11.96	60-80 lbs	$120	$108.04
Zinnia (Flowers)	-	4 transplants	$9.96	Multiple blooms	$125	$115.04
Marigold (Flowers)	-	4 transplants	$11.56	Multiple blooms	-	
Nasturtium (Flowers)	-	4 transplants	$11.56	Multiple blooms	-	

Significant Other Sway-Sheet

Growers Garden

Beets (Red)	100 ft	2 packets	$5.98	60-80 lbs	$100	$94.02
Broccoli	100 ft	16 transplants	$55.84	100 heads	$349	$293.16
Cabbage	100 ft	2 transplants (6 plants each)	$55.84	100 heads	$349	$293.16
Parsley	100 ft	4 plants	$8.00	224 bunches	$225	$217
Carrots	100 ft	2 packets	$5.98	80-100 lbs	$150	$144.02
Tomatoes	100ft	10 packs (6 plants per pack)	$209.40	600-800 lbs	$1,000	$790.60
Squash	100 ft	4 packets	$11.96	60-80 squash	$100	$88.04
Basil	100 ft	1 seed packet	$2.99	224 bunches	$450	$447.01
Arugula	100 ft	2 packets	$5.98	40-60 lbs	$80	$74.02
Radicchio	100 ft	1 packet	$2.99	20-40 heads	$80	$77.01
Peas	100 ft	4 packs	$11.96	40lbs	$80	$69.04
Anmaranth	100 ft	1 pack	$2.99	blooms		
Endive	100 ft	4 packs	$11.96	40 heads	$100	$88.04
Potatoes	100 ft	10 lbs	$12	100 lbs+	$200	$188
Total			$544.79		$4,608	$3967

Significant Other Sway-Sheet

Growers Garden

Beets (Red)	100ft	2 packets	$5.98	60-80 lbs	$100	$94.02
Broccoli	100ft	16 transplants	$55.84	100 heads	$349	$293.16
Cabbage	100ft	2 transplants (6 plants each)	$55.84	100 heads	$349	$293.16
Parsley	100ft	4 plants	$8.00	224 bunches	$225	$217
Carrots	100ft	2 packets	$5.98	80-100 lbs	$150	$144.02
Tomatoes	100ft	10 packs (6 plants per pack)	$209.40	600-800 lbs	$1,000	$790.60
Squash	100ft	4 packets	$11.96	60-80 squash	$100	$88.04
Basil	100ft	1 seed packet	$2.99	224 bunches	$450	$447.01
Arugula	100ft	2 packets	$5.98	40-60 lbs	$80	$74.02
Radicchio	100ft	1 packet	$2.99	20-40 heads	$80	$77.01
Peas	100ft	4 packs	$11.96	40lbs	$80	$69.04
Anmaranth	100ft	1 pack	$2.99	blooms		
Endive	100ft	4 packs	$11.96	40heads	$100	$88.04

A few things to keep in mind: Preparing the Grower's Garden (our largest layout) will take more than fifteen minutes a day—especially if you're starting from uncut sod. Plan for a solid weekend setup with two people working eight hours to get the beds in place. Once established, most weekly maintenance tasks can fit into fifteen-minute daily windows. However, harvesting and food storage will require additional time.

You can absolutely tuck food preservation into small pockets throughout the season. That's how we do it—because life is full. I've canned over 500 jars in nap-time hours or in the two hours after dinner. It's manageable and fits our busy schedule. That said, if I'm learning a new technique or trying something new, I prefer to block out a larger stretch of time. Otherwise, the session can feel rushed and stressful. One helpful strategy: Set aside one day a month, from July through October, for processing vegetables—whether that's freezing, canning, or fermenting. A little planning goes a long way.

Reminder: Free is great—but it often costs in time or quality. Be honest about your budget and goals. If your aim is to save time and reduce frustration, invest in quality materials—especially soil and raised beds. These two components have a lasting impact on your garden's success.

And Most of All—Stay Consistent

A little effort each day adds up. The payoff for your time, planning, and upfront investment is real food, right outside your door. You are building something that will bless your family for years to come.

Don't forget the most important step: harvest your garden. It will grow. Stay with it. Keep showing up. The return is coming.

ITEMS NEEDED   COST

SAVINGS

Bonus Tips for Saving Money
- Buy seeds in bulk or split packets with friends.
- Use EBT benefits to purchase seeds
- Save seeds from heirloom varieties
- Visit seed libraries in your area.
- Repurpose materials for garden beds.
- Look for local free or low-cost soil.

Step 2: Choosing Your Garden Location

Now that you've decided on a budget and a garden plan, let's pick the perfect spot. This step does not take a lot of time but it does require that you are home or are able to view your potential spot, once an hour, for 8-12 hrs.

Estimated Time: 10-15 minutes (A couple of minutes to scope out your potential site and then one minute every hour for eight hours to "sun-stalk" your yard).

The Perfect Garden Location Checklist

- **Look for the Green:** Is your lawn lush, dry, soggy, and pooling with water? Stony? Is it full of weeds? Healthy grass usually means healthy soil. Look for the greenest spot.
- **Sunlight:** Plants need 8–12 hours of direct sunlight to thrive. Do you have trees surrounding your area? If it is uncontested full sun you are good to go. If there are trees, houses, or shrubs, note the chart below. Snap a picture of your yard on your phone, use the edit feature, or print it. Draw lines to mark how the shadows move throughout the day.
- **Drainage:** Is water sticking around? Find a spot where water drains well. If your yard gets puddles that linger too long, it's not the right place.
- **Accessibility:** The closer your garden is to your house, the more likely you'll stay on top of weeding and care. You don't want your first garden far from the house.
- **Space to Dream:** Leave room for paths. It's not essential, but if you mulch a border around the garden it looks so much more "finished" and keeps weeds from growing right up next to your bed. At the very least, leave enough room to mow between the beds. You don't want to only be able to weed whack that space.
- **Use twine and stakes** to mark out your new garden.

Observe Your Space

Track sunlight at different times of the day ideal peek every hour but at minimum morning, midday, and afternoon.

Note shaded areas from trees, buildings, or fences.

Observe how light shifts throughout the seasons.

Time

How Much Sun?

Nearly all fruiting veggies will do best in full sun.

Full Sun (8+ hours) – Best for tomatoes, peppers, squash, and melons.

Partial Sun (4-6 hours) – Good for root crops, herbs, and some flowers.

Partial Shade (2-4 hours) – Ideal for leafy greens, lettuce, and brassicas.

Full Shade (Less than 2 hours) – Limited options, but can work for ferns or shade-tolerant edibles like mint.

Watch shade from house

Watch for shade from tree

Perfect Spot

8-12 hrs of sun
Close to house
Outside of shade zone
Not rocky
Not prone to flooding

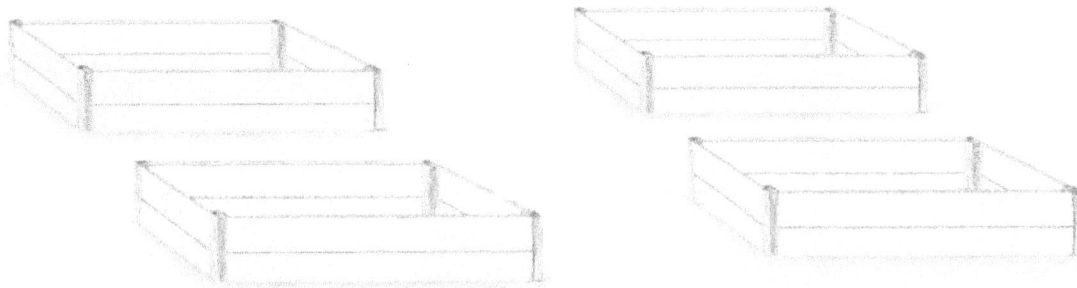

You're almost there!

Step 3: Seed Selection and Sourcing

There are so many places to get seeds. I mention a few below that I have relied on for years. I love working with them. Please note, no matter where you shop, there are some things to think about when considering seeds:

- Regionally adapted—seeds grown for your climate will always perform better, especially for regions with weather extremes.
- Price—Cheap seeds are a waste of time. Poor germination from shady seeds is so disappointing.

Bulk is not always better. Aim to mostly buy what you can grow in a year while you are figuring out what you need. I have found that too many seeds lead to overwhelm and overwhelm leads to inaction. If you are a couple seasons in then go for it. You know what you like and you know what performs well.

Seed Shopping—My Favorites: Get on these guys' mailing lists!

- **Botanical Interests:** Great for beginners! Their packets are not only beautiful but packed with clear instructions. These seed packets are worthy of saving as a mini-reference year after year.
- **True Leaf Market:** Think Costco for seeds but way more fun to browse. Great for buying in bulk. Their seed packets do not offer instructions and the labels tend to fade so mark well.
- **High Mountain Mowing:** Amazing for tomatoes and onions, and their customer service is so friendly you'll want to send them a thank-you card. I also love that while they are not overly flowery, they give you the basic info right on the packet.

Seeds at a Discount

- **Dollar Store Seeds:** I pass if I need good results. Cheap, yes—but a gamble when it comes to germination.
- **Spring and Fall sales:** GREAT OPTION. Seed prices tend to remain pretty consistent throughout the year, but you'll notice some sales pop up around the end of November and as we head into the growing seasons in the early spring. No matter how tempting a deal may be, make sure you're choosing a seed company that is reputable and is known for providing varieties for your specific climate. A "good deal" becomes a terrible deal when the seeds don't sprout consistently or if the seeds just are not suited to your region.

- **Seed libraries**—These allow you to "borrow" seeds, plant them, and then let one of the plants go to seed, saving the new seeds to return to the library. These free seeds open up a world of possibilities for community growers and are they more reliable than some sources simply because the people who take time to save seeds are passionate about growing.

Note: Seed libraries aren't always tested for viability. You want to do that before sowing. You can check the likelihood of germination with a simple float test. To perform the test, fill a small bowl with water and place your seeds in it. After 10-15minutes, observe the seeds: those that **sink** are generally viable, while those that **float** may be dead or damaged. For more accurate results, you can also perform a germination test. Simply place a few seeds on a damp paper towel, fold it over, and keep it in a warm place. Check daily and up to a week for sprouting—seeds that don't sprout may be less viable. This method works for most seeds, though some, like beans and peas, can also be tested using the float method. I would call this a free but not fifteen-minute friendly option.

Deep River Girls' Tea

Believe 24hrs is enough!

Our first garden didn't have flowers. While I got a harvest and was thrilled, it wasn't abundant.

As I researched more, I learned that flowers were not space hogs—they drew in pollinators, repelled pests, and added beauty. Ever since, flowers have played a large role in my garden beds, bringing beauty, and bees.

Garden Thyme Checks

Learning to Grow

- [ ] Pick out budget
- [ ] Scout Your Yard: Set a timer and check each spot hourly to see where the sun shines most.
- [ ] Check Drainage: Watch where water flows after it rains. If puddles stick around, find a better spot.
- [ ] Sketch It Out: Grab a notebook and quickly sketch a layout of your future garden (paths, plants, etc.), or pick a plan from the back of this book.
- [ ] Seed Window Shopping: Fill out the Veggies We Eat form. Browse catalogs or websites and pick 3–5 varieties you know you want to grow. We'll complete our seed order at the end of the book.
- [ ] Test Run Tools: Find your trowel, gloves, and garden journal. (Bonus points if you find last year's notes!)
- [ ] High-Five Yourself: You're officially on your way to garden greatness. Keep it up!

Deep River Girls' Tea
Plant Beauty

I started falling in love with the garden when I was still small.
I'll never forget standing in the shadow of a sunflower that was taller than I was,
its bright, cheerful face following the sun across the sky.
It amazed me that something so small, something I had planted with my own
hands, could grow into something so massive, towering above me like that.
To this day, sunflowers are still one of my favorite flowers
— Keira

Tools I Wouldn't Trade

I am a minimalist at heart. There are so many tools that will make your life easier, but like everything else more options lead to overwhelm if you are not really clear about why and how a tool is needed. Ultimately, the most effective tool will be your own two hands. If dirty fingernails are not your thing, the second most important thing will be to invest in a pair of gloves that are comfortable and durable but also thin enough so you can still handle tiny seeds. That said, there are tools that amazingly simplify gardening. Here is a list of tools I think every gardener should have no matter the stage:

Small Items

- Hand pruners—Pick the best you can afford. I love to have a medium pair (best for pruning large stems and vines) and a small pair (best for trimming yearly tomato suckers, onion tops, and herbs). Pro tip: Snag a tool belt or thick apron with large pockets—you'll want to keep these close but not cut-a-hole-in-your-jean-pocket close.
- Hand trowel—You'll be able to slice through stubborn roots, twine, and spent plant material as well as mark rows for sowing seeds.
- Zip ties and tomato clips—You will need something to hold your plants to your trellis system. Tomato clips are gentler than zip ties, and they come in compostable varieties.
- Twine and stakes—For marking beds. Twine can also be used for trellising.
- **Labels for plants**—Yes, you will need them. Think Tape and a Sharpie works, or Amazon has plastic labels on the cheap (and if you figure out a way to keep little ones from losing them, please share!).
- **Ruler**—for spacing plants (your hand works too but there are plenty of sales in September).

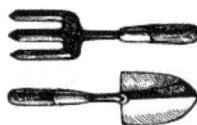

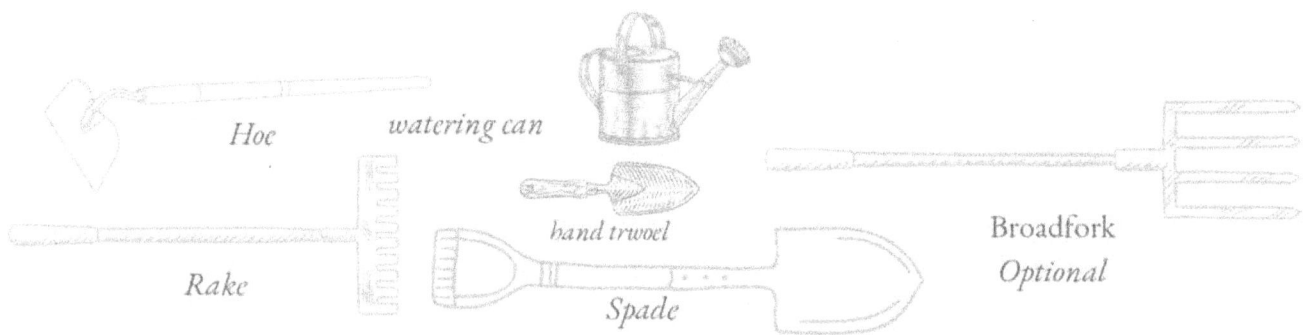

Hoe   *watering can*

Rake   *hand trwoel*   Broadfork
Spade   *Optional*

Large Items

- Spade—Everyone needs a good garden shovel. You won't need it often for four raised beds so borrowing one may work fine, but you do need something.
- Garden rake—For smoothing garden beds and raking mulch. Choose strong, firm tines.
- Wheelbarrow or garden cart—Essential. This tool will be your go-to for soil, harvesting, kiddie rides, end-of-season weeding, and carting prunings to compost.
- Raised Beds—There are many options out there. Here are some key things to look for:
  - Ease of assembly
  - Height— 2ft is ideal, do not go lower than 18" for ample root growth.
  - Wood—Natural material, but prone to rotting. Watch out because pallets can be preserved with chemicals that are toxic to your garden or made with wood that rots quickly. Cedar and locust are my favorite options.
  - Metal—Watch for sharp edges. Especially if your home has kids, you want a raised bed that is made with materials that can handle young helpers (sturdy) and has no sharp edges (safe).
  - Formless raised beds—these are more difficult to maintain. What you save in money, you pay for in time and maintenance. The soil can only be effectively mounded by about 6 in., so the ground should be broadforked before you add your layers. This is by far the cheapest option, and one we have used frequently.

Pro-tip: Ana White has decent beginner plans for free on her website, I would just add more height to make them reach 18"-24".

Also, the best Mother's Day gift I ever received was a good-quality dumpcart. Just sayin'.

- **Optional (But oh-so-convenient):**
  - Broadfork: A luxury that is especially useful the first year. Essential for the no-till 3,000 square-foot garden plans.
  - Watering timer: Automating watering comes with drawbacks, but the convenience is sweet.
  - Soaker hoses. If you see these items on sale, or a good deal at a garage sale or Facebook Marketplace, snap them up!

What You'll Need (That Money Can't Buy)

You are making so much progress. You've set your budget and selected your tools. Now what else is there to make this year's garden a success?

- Grit: For the messy, heavy jobs. Think of grit as your ability to dig in, even when bugs, bad weather, or just poor attitudes make you want to quit. Remember: Grit doesn't quit. Grit gets gritty.
- Perseverance: When mistakes happen (and they most assuredly will), commit to finishing what you start. This is the mindset that rolls up its sleeves when others fold.
- Wonder: Gardening is a miracle-don't lose sight of that. Be the person who never forgets that the miracle of life is the greatest mystery we can plunge our hands into and participate in.

Something I borrowed from Jessica Seward *(Roots and Refuge)* for when a seed first emerges is celebrating a seed's birthday. Jessica has inspired my love of tomatoes since almost day one. I love the imagery and the rhythm of celebration the word creates. The day a seed pokes its head out of the soil allowing us to see what has been long hidden is so precious. I hope we all pause and savor the little "birthdays," because it is the little things we mark that keep wonder and gratitude alive in our gardens.

Soil

The final pillar in our prep season is soil. You cannot garden without eventually falling in love with dirt. Soil is where it all begins. The top 12 inches are essential for plant life, supporting everything from nutrient transfer to organic breakdown to healthy growth. If you splurge anywhere, splurge on the quality of soil you bring to your garden.

Good soil is typically a rich, dark brown or black color, which indicates it is full of organic matter, such as composted material and decomposing plant material. It is moist-you can take a handful, and it feels like a wrung-out sponge.

What Makes Soil "Good"?

Let's get a little techy with dirt. Do you ever wonder why some plants thrive while others do not? (So do I!) Perhaps you question what is so special about rotting veggies (compost) that has gardeners always talking about it? The life of the soil is more complex and mind-boggling than a middle school romance—but let's break it down. (See what I did there?)

- **Topsoil:** Topsoil is the nutrient-rich, uppermost layer of soil where most plant growth occurs. It's made up of a mixture of organic material, minerals, and microorganisms that support plant health and productivity. This layer is crucial for providing plants with the nutrients and structure they need to thrive.

- **Nutrients**: Like humans, plants need a balanced diet to thrive. Compost adds magnesium, nitrogen, potassium, phosphorus, boron, etc. back into the soil.

- **Composted Material**: Broken-down organic matter, like leaves, grass clippings, and food scraps enrich the soil, improving fertility and structure. Tough, dry crumbly soil usually means it needs more compost. When your soil is alive with freshly broken-down matter, it serves your plants a farm-to-table buffet that is deeply nourishing. The organic matter not only adds essential nutrients but also improves soil texture, making it easier for plant roots to grow. Additionally, it acts like a sponge, helping the soil retain moisture, so your plants stay hydrated longer, even in dry conditions. Over time, this creates a healthy, thriving soil ecosystem that supports strong, vibrant plant growth.

- **Worm Castings and Soil Life**: Healthy soil teems with life. Worms, microbes, and insects recycle nutrients, making them available to plants. Worm castings are nutrient-rich and signify healthy soil.

- **Beneficial Fungi and Microbes**: Mycorrhizal fungi and other microorganisms connect plants to soil nutrients, playing a critical role in nutrient absorption.

Eating Ice Cubes: Understanding pH and NPK.

The simplest explanation is that pH measures whether your soil is acidic, neutral, or alkaline. Neutral soil has a pH of 7.0, while soil with a pH below 7.0 is acidic ("sour") and above 7.0 is alkaline ("basic"). The ideal range for most plants is slightly acidic to neutral, between 6.0 and 7.0.

Why is this important? Plants can only absorb certain nutrients when the soil's pH is in the optimal range. Think of it this way: If you dump a bunch of ice cubes in the soil, your plants still get dehydrated. Why? Frozen water doesn't nourish your plants. This is why a tundra, like Antarctica, can be full of "water" (ice)and still be considered a desert. Conversely, if you try to "water" your garden with steam, it doesn't work either. Water needs to be in the right form and temperature to benefit your plants.

Similarly, when soil's pH is in the right range (6.0–7.0), nutrients are in their most available form for plants. If the pH dips below 6.0, your soil develops "heartburn." While phosphorus becomes less available in acidic conditions, trace minerals like iron, manganese, boron, copper, and zinc become more soluble and, in some cases, overly available—potentially to toxic levels and "burn" plant roots. Symptoms like stunted growth or leaf damage (like curling leaves)may result, especially for plants sensitive to excess manganese or aluminum found in very acidic soil.

On the flip side, if pH rises above 7.0, those trace minerals "freeze". In alkaline conditions, essential nutrients like iron, manganese, boron, copper, and zinc become chemically bound and unavailable to plants. Signs of nutrient deficiencies in alkaline soils include yellowing leaves (chlorosis), splitting root vegetables, scabbing, and general stunted growth. If you follow our guide to filling your raised beds, you should have no problems with pH but if you want to determine your soil pH, you can do a soil test!

NPK: The Miracle Minerals

Soil tests also reveal nutrient deficiencies and imbalances. Plants need a balance of nutrients to grow strong and healthy. Think of it like a healthy diet for your garden, e ept the main "food groups" for the garden are NPK : Nitrogen (N), Phosphorus (P), and Potassium (K). This is important to know because those bottles of organic fertilizers you may need mid-season have "NPK" concentrations listed in different proportions to meet your garden's specific needs. When you understand why these nutrients are important you can make informed decisions about your fertilizer needs. Let's break down what each does:

- **Nitrogen (N):** Essential for leafy growth, it acts like protein for plants. Be mindful of overuse, as it encourages excessive leaf growth at the expense of fruit.
- **Phosphorus (P):** Crucial for root and flower development, it supports healthy root systems and blooming. This means your root veggies are going to need a little more of this.
- **Potassium (K):** Enhances overall plant health, helping resist diseases and endure harsh conditions.

RECAP and Takeaways

- **Balance is crucial:** Excessive nitrogen can lead to yellowing plants, "burnt", while insufficient phosphorus can hinder blooming.
- **pH:** Soil must be between 6-7 pH for optimal plant health.
- **Good soil = happy plants:** Nutrient-rich soil sets the foundation for a flourishing garden.
- Use your **soil test** to pinpoint what your soil needs at the beginning and/or end of your growing season.
- Robust fruiting plants called "**heavy feeder**s" depend on **Nitrogen** to produce.
- All your root veggies are going to need a little extra **Phosphorus** to prosper.
- **Potassium** is one of the key nutrients along with calcium that support strong stem growth.
- Balanced soil=happy plants

Minimal-Till Soil Prep

No-till methods allow beneficial organisms like earthworms, fungi, and microbes to thrive. By preserving the soil's natural structure, you're creating a thriving ecosystem that promotes long-term soil health, better water retention, and fewer weeds. Plus, with the deep bedding method, weed control becomes much easier and far less labor-intensive. It's a win-win for your plants and you!

With raised bed gardening, you build your garden right on top of the existing grass—no tilling required. I recommend starting in the fall and letting the bed sit over the winter, but there's really no wrong time to start a garden—unless, of course, it's during a blizzard; that might be a little tricky! In all seriousness, in all zones you can get ready in any season and then plant what is appropriate for your season or wait until spring.

Option 1: Quick and Costly-

The easiest option is going to be making a phone call to a local supplier and getting 4-5 yards of raised bed garden soil mix. Line the bottom of the bed with cardboard. This smothers the grass and gives the worms living in the soil their favorite food to eat. Make sure the cardboard is plain brown, with minimal writing. Next fill the raised bed with purchased raised bed mix or garden mix soil. This is by far the easiest option, but it is not cheap. Note if doing a frameless raised bed or a shallower raised bed frame, the breakdown of the cardboard will rob nutrients from the plants.

Option 2: Simplified Method

Fill the bed using:
- ⅓ **wood chips, sticks, vegetable waste, and grass clippings**.
- ⅓ **composted manure**
- ⅓ **purchased "Organic Garden Mix" soil.**

You must have 8-12 inches of purchased raised bed mix for the best results.

Optional: Top with 1 cubic foot seed-starting mix per 4x8 bed to retain moisture. Young seeds need a balanced seed bed.

The gardener's art is in those top 12 inches—a canvas of endless potential."
—Lisa Mason Ziegler

GOOD SOIL

Good garden soil is rich, dark, and crumbly, indicating a healthy balance of organic matter, minerals, and moisture. It holds water without becoming soggy and drains well to prevent root rot. When you squeeze it, it should clump slightly but not mold like clay or crumble like sand. You need signs of good structure and life. Healthy soil smells earthy and has a thriving ecosystem of microbes and worms. Soil is your most important crop.

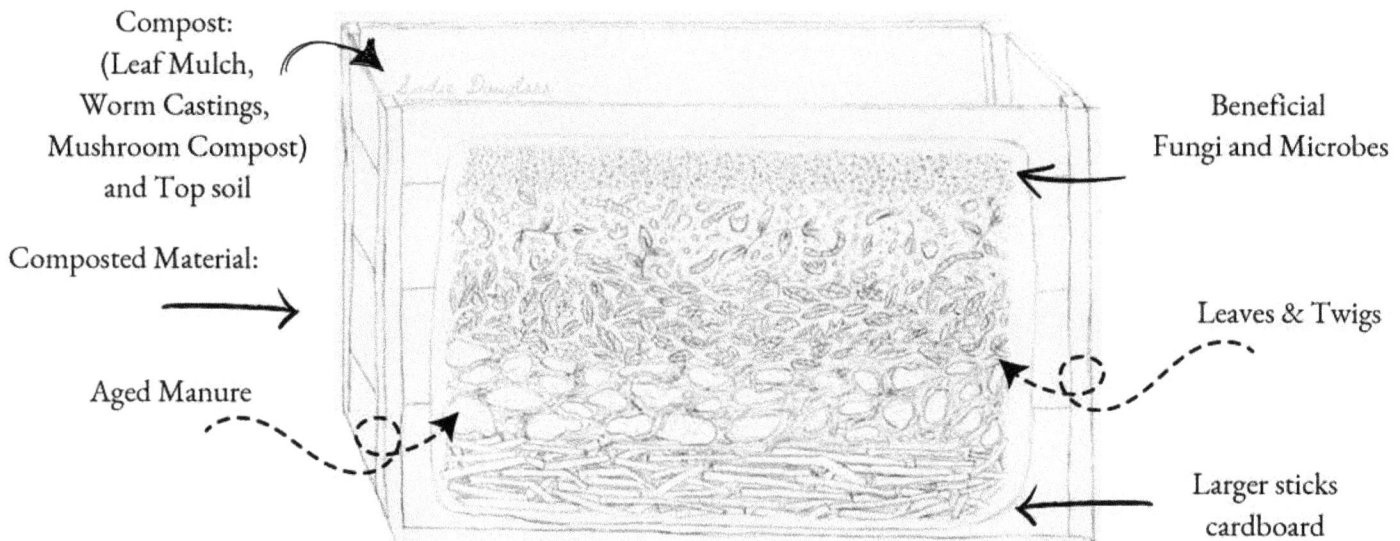

Compost:
(Leaf Mulch,
Worm Castings,
Mushroom Compost)
and Top soil

Composted Material:

Aged Manure

Beneficial
Fungi and Microbes

Leaves & Twigs

Larger sticks
cardboard

Raised Bed Formula (Layering Technique)

To create the ideal soil for your raised beds or garden, you'll need a balanced mix of organic materials. Layer these materials as you build your bed, like a garden "lasagna." This layering method helps create rich, healthy soil while minimizing disturbance to soil life. The beauty of no-till gardening is that it eliminates the hard work of renting or buying a machine to break up the ground or the huge time investment of digging the soil by hand—and let's be honest, who doesn't want less work?

You can save money by sourcing free or cheap raised bed "filling" and mixing your own raised bed lasagna. This comes with some warnings. Try to find out as much as you can before using. Be aware that you can run the risk of introducing toxins or pesticides by using unscreened sources. With those disclaimers out of the way, I will say, there have been many years we simply needed our resources to be free. I get it. It may not be the "best" but whether purchased or sourced for free, we do our best, say a prayer, and trust God with the rest.

Let's Build It

1. 6 in. Cardboard/Woody Materials: Lay down a layer of cardboard to block weeds and decompose into soil.
2. 3 in. Manure Compost: Provides nitrogen to break down cardboard and support lush growth. You want this to be thoroughly aged.
3. 4 in. Leaves/Grass Clippings: spent veggies, weeds that have not gone to seed and will not multiply by runners. Add organic matter to enhance soil structure.
4. 6 in. Topsoil: Establishes a good growing medium for plant roots.
5. 6 in. Compost: Rich in N, P, and K, it supports plant root development. Bonus: Top with seed starting mix for moisture retention.

Supplies You'll Need:
- A shovel
- A wheelbarrow
- Approximately 29 cubic feet of garden mix soil, or mix your own

You can fill a single raised bed in about 15 minutes. You can stretch the project out over four days or dedicate an afternoon. Remember it's about consistency and progress.

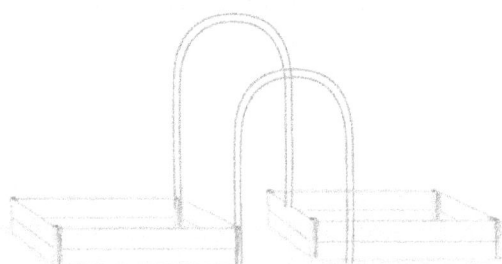

RAISED BEDS

FRAMELESS RAISED BED

The Little Garden Bed That Could

Don't forget that while these gardens may look different, they both can grow the exact same amount of food. Frameless raised beds are accessible for any budget and are much more scaleable.

I love the look of framed beds. There are so many reasons why they work so well. At the end of the day, done is better than perfect. If money is tight, get creative and enjoy the fruits of your labor.

Reality check

If you're building beds from scrap lumber and hauling free wood chips in five-gallon buckets—that's not a 15-minute task. Building and filling your beds is one area where the 15-minute rule might bend a little, simply because it's more efficient to tackle this as a project in an afternoon rather than spreading it out over several days. Shoveling a wheelbarrow full of wood chips or delivered compost can be broken into 15 minute chunks but you may rather just get it done all at once. Bottom line–do what works for you and stay consistent.

I am committed to the 15-minute promise: there are many "plug-and-play" raised bed kits that drop into place and can be assembled quickly. But if you're going the DIY route with scrap wood, how much time it takes depends on your handiness level and the ease of sourcing materials.

I've spent countless hours filling totes and buckets with dirt while my kids played nearby—and sometimes, they even helped! Sometimes the cheapest to the wallet costs us the most in time. I want to share both. **Everything** in this garden can be done in 15 minutes but unfortunately I can't promise everything fast will be free.

Chapter Recap:

You have a garden!!!

This Prep Season is all about starting small, taking calm, purposeful steps, and celebrating each little victory along the way. You've got this—and I'm cheering you on as you begin this beautiful gardening journey. Do you want a simple guide to break these steps down into daily tasks? See Part 3 for a 36-day comprehensive guide to starting your first garden. Check out Section 3. It's a no-fail gift to get you growing.

Garden Thyme Checks

Build It

- [ ] Raised Bed Setup (15 minutes each):

  Mark and Prepare Your Garden Beds

  Measure your space. Leave 3 feet between beds and a 2-foot border around the garden perimeter.

- [ ] Lay down plain brown cardboard over the entire area and wet it thoroughly.

  Use a free source of wood chips (ChipDrop or your town's recycling program) to surround your beds.

  Break this into smaller tasks:

  - [ ] Order chips

  - [ ] Order manure, topsoil, and compost

  - [ ] Spread chips and soil

  Gather Supplies (15-minute blocks)

- [ ] Locate sources for these essentials:

  Compost

  Topsoil

  Manure

  Wood chips

- [ ] Assemble Raised Beds (15 minute minimum per bed)

> **Pro tip:** Slide-together wooden varieties or quality metal beds are amazing and fast. Two people can whip one together in 15 minutes. Bigger builds will cost more time.

Plant Season

"I am excessively fond of a cottage; there is always so much comfort, so much elegance about them. And I protest, if I had any money to spare, I should buy a little land and build one myself..."

Sense and Sensibility, Jane Austen

SOW SUCCESSFUL
THE BEGINNER'S GUIDE TO VEGGIES

Whether you're a first-time gardener or a seasoned green thumb, starting with a basic overview of the veggies you are growing sets the stage for success. In this chapter, we'll cover seed selection and sowing, and introduce a fail-proof *Family-Friends-Foe* planting method. We round it out with key techniques for watering and fertilization.

You'll complete our *"Veggies We Eat"* form and pick a custom-designed garden bed, tailored to your goals. For beginners, I recommend starting simple—use one of our pre-designed planting plans and use this as a reference section. For those of you with a few seasons under your belt, pull out your garden catalog and your garden list. You are about to design your best garden yet.

Thyme Check Pause -

- **Fill Out the *"Veggies We Eat"*** form at the end of this section. If you did not do this before, do it now. Normally we do a Thyme Check at the end of the chapter but you can't do the next step until you've considered what you want to grow. Take a moment and highlight 8-12 of your favorites to fill your 4x8 beds.
- **Fast option**: Skip the choices. Pick one of our garden plans from the back and keep reading.

The Basics

Key Vocabulary
- **Germination** (that's when a seed begins to grow) is a seed's birthday! Requires that seeds are placed at the right depth and in the right conditions. If a seed is planted too deep it may never reach the surface or too shallow and it could dry out or fail to root properly.
- **Sow**: To plant seeds in the soil. A simple task and one of the most fun. A basic rule of thumb is to sow seeds twice as deep as their size. So, tiny seeds like carrots, onions, and kale are planted closer to the surface of the soil, as they don't need much space to germinate. On the other hand, larger seeds

like beans and beets should be pressed into the soil to ensure they have enough room to grow and establish strong roots.

- **Cultivate**: This refers to working the soil. It's a term I use to describe disturbing the top layer of soil to prevent weeds from sprouting.

- **Amend**: To amend the soil is to add something that improves it, usually something rich in nutrients. Most often, we amend the soil with compost.

- **Mulch**: This is a covering placed on top of the soil, which can be made of wood chips, crushed leaves, grass clippings, or even stones. Mulch has its pros and cons. It locks in moisture, suppresses weeds, and regulates soil temperature. On the flip side, there can be too much of a good thing with mulch. Locked in moisture can fester disease. Mulch can tie up nutrients as it breaks down, resulting in erratic production because of inconsistencies in the soil. My rule of thumb: mulch paths and amend beds with thoroughly finished compost. I don't ever put wood chips on top of raised beds because that saps nutrients.

- **Living Mulch**: These are plants that grow lower to the ground like spinach, thyme, and marigolds that can act as living mulch. They provide natural shade for the soil, preventing weed seeds from sprouting and helping to hold moisture in the ground. Another example of a low-growing plant is lettuce.

Plant Pairing Made Easy

You've got your budget sorted, your plan chosen, your beds built and your soil mastered. Now comes the big question: What do I grow? Enter the real MVP of garden planning: The "Friend, Foe, and Family" system. This approach simplifies designing a thriving garden, no matter its size or location.

When I first started gardening, I hesitated to grow flowers, thinking I didn't have the space. But once I added marigolds and zinnias, everything changed. Not only did my garden look beautiful, but my vegetable yields improved dramatically. Pollinators swarmed in, the garlic and onions that surrounded my garden helped deter pests, and I started harvesting more in less space.

The "Friend, Foe, and Family" System

Permaculture and Organic explained. If you're not familiar with permaculture, there are many philosophies and approaches within the concept. At its core, permaculture focuses on creating systems where everything works together in harmony. Waste is minimized, and the ecosystem thrives. While organic principles focus primarily on eliminating chemicals and genetically modified seeds, they don't emphasize interplanting or other methods as strongly as permaculture does. Permaculture encourages designing gardens that foster interdependence among plants, animals, and the environment.

The common ground between the two approaches is that both aim to maintain soil and plant health by working with natural cycles. Instead of relying on artificial inputs, they focus on creating systems where plants, soil, and ecosystems are self-sustaining. When we apply these ideas to garden design, our garden beds thrive by utilizing nature's inherent rhythms. This is an extremely simplified explanation of two complex topics. These are the fundamental principals for the 15 Minute Method.

15 Minute Companion Planting Method

Friends (beneficial plant pairings) align with both organic and permaculture principles by promoting natural pest control, enhancing plant health, and encouraging biodiversity. For example, basil and tomatoes are a classic pairing, where basil helps repel pests like aphids and enhances tomato flavor, all without the need for chemical pesticides or fertilizers. These partnerships help keep the everything balanced and healthy, an essential part of both organic and permaculture methods.

Foes (plants that don't work well together): Some plants compete for resources or attract pests harmful to their neighbors. By observing these interactions, gardeners can reduce the need for artificial interventions and minimize plant stress. For example, peppers and tomatoes both need high levels of nitrogen and share similar pests, which means they shouldn't be planted too close together.Recognizing these competitive relationships allows for better planning, ensuring that plants don't deplete the same resources and that the garden remains diverse and healthy.

Family (plants of the same botanical family: While plants in the same family often grow well together, grouping them too closely can increase the risk of pest and disease spread. Understanding these dynamics helps gardeners design systems that optimize plant health by considering both the benefits and potential risks of plant relationships. Ultimately, this creates a more resilient garden where plant health is supported by thoughtful design.

1. **Pick Your Star:** Choose a primary plant, typically one that takes up the most space or produces fruit like tomatoes.
2. **Find Their Friends:** Add companion plants like basil and onions to support growth and deter pests.
3. **Add Pollinators:** Include flowers like marigolds that attract pollinators and provide pest control.
4. **Fill the Gaps:** Add low-maintenance, fast-growing crops like lettuce or radishes.

For Example, in a **tomato-focused** 4x8 bed row, one would have 4 tomato plants as the star. In a row 18 inches from the tomatoes, I would plant 3 basil and 3 marigolds or zinnias, and next, I would end with a low-growing filler like lettuce.

Or a beginner-friendly **lettuce bed** (super low-maintenance) could include 2 rows of radishes for a quick crop followed by rainbow chard mixed with mellow-colored dwarf zinnias for additional color while the chard provides a green that stands up in summer heat. Next, carrots at the center which take longer to mature and remain need to remain undisturbed. A row of alternating red and green lettuce heads backed by spring-sown shallots.

The opportunities are endless when you know what you want to grow and how to shape beautiful beds of varying heights and colors.

Gardening is both an art and a science. The more you learn about plant families and relationships, the better you'll get at designing beds. For your first year, stick with the plans in the back and take notes on what works. The next chapter will look in detail over the most commonly grown veggies. As you read about the different families, remember you don't have to memorize everything. There are plenty of charts and plans in the back to keep you growing for years to come. As long as you know the families, with a few exceptions, you can safely swap out members of the same family, i.e. you can swap cucumbers with mellons on the trellis and not need to make other adjustments to the plan. Before we close out this chapter, let's just cover some universal care topics.

FERTILIZING:

FEEDING YOUR GARDEN RIGHT

Your plants aren't just thirsty—they're hungry too. Feeding them properly keeps them strong and productive. Compost will be your best friend but it takes time to establish a weed-free supply. Compost adds life to your soil by introducing microorganisms and organic matter, enhancing its overall quality. If your soil is sandy or clay-like, mixing in compost will help improve its consistency and create a better balance. Compost is by far the most sustainable fertilizer, being made with all-natural repurposed waste materials.

Fertilizer Tips

- Option 1: For heavy feeders, apply organic liquid fertilizers weekly, following package directions. Some brands I use are listed in the back.

- Option 2: Side-dress with granular fertilizers when blossoms appear and just before fruit sets to boost yields.

- Avoid Overdoing It: Over-fertilizing, especially early, can harm plants. When in doubt, less is more.

A Word About Pests

Pests are just insects we haven't found a purpose for—yet. Bees are critical pollinators, while slugs and centipedes help decompose organic matter (even if they snack on your leaves). Instead of reaching for broad-spectrum pesticides that kill everything, try a gentler approach. Remember that prevention is key. For stubborn pests like tomato hornworms and potato bugs, hand-picking is a game-changer. Take a small bucket of soapy water on your daily garden stroll and pluck the offenders right off your plants. It's straightforward, effective, and completely pesticide-free. Once a plant is infested, it is really hard to overcome.

- **Soapy Water Walks:** During mid-summer, take a few minutes each day to shake leaves, check for eggs, and dip infested foliage into a jar of soapy water. For leaves that are badly damaged, prune them entirely.

- **Diatomaceous Earth:** Can be used for stubborn pests like potato beetles but it's a broad-spectrum solution that also kills beneficial organisms. It can help if you have a bad infestation, but use with caution.

- **Consistency is Key:** Pests and diseases thrive in gardens left unattended. By dedicating just 15 minutes a day, you can tackle issues early, saving time and money on unnecessary products.
- **Prevention by Design:** Elevated garden beds deter many pests. Companion planting acts as a natural repellent, and daily check-ins keep your garden in tip-top shape.

Basic Care

Watering: You want your soil to feel like a wrung-out sponge. Water when dry and skip when soggy.

Early Days:
Water lightly every day to keep the topsoil moist for germinating seeds and young plants (usually first 2 weeks). Once plants are established (about two weeks or when true leaves appear), reduce watering slightly to allow the soil to dry between sessions. This encourages deeper root growth, making plants stronger and more resilient. You don't want to stress the plant and cause it to wilt or dry out.

Deep Watering:
After plants are established, (about three weeks), switch to deep watering once or twice a week depending on weather (more frequently in warmer climates). This encourages roots to grow even deeper, leading to healthier, drought-resistant plants.

A. M. Water. This is best. Plants have what they need to remain unstressed throughout the day.

P. M. Water Plant perks up but most plants to do not like to be super wet over night (unless you live in zones 7+). Dampness attracts pest and fungus.

No Water Hot Day
Plants can recover from occasional water delays but repeatedly stressed plants do do not bear good fruit and are prone to disease.

"Opportunity is missed by most people because it is dressed in overalls and looks like work."
— Thomas A. Edison

Garden Allies

Not all bugs are bad! Beneficial insects like ladybugs, lacewings, and parasitic wasps are natural predators of garden pests. Attract these allies with flowers like marigolds, calendula, and yarrow. These plants provide habitats for your helpers and keep the ecosystem balanced.

WHAT HAVE YOU SEEN?

Lady Bug:

Good guy, eats aphids

Praying Mantis:

Good guy, eats other insects.

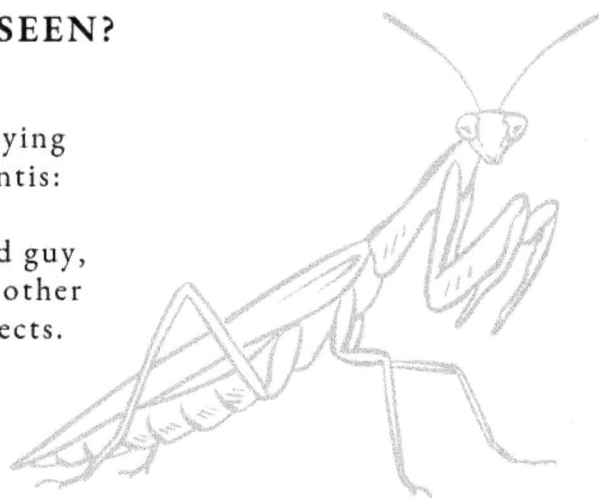

Remember that it's bugs out of balance that is a bad thing. You need insects in your garden

Toads:

Not an insect but they eat slugs and other bugs.

Honey Bee

Pollinator

Disease Control Tips

While pests get the spotlight, disease prevention is equally crucial for a thriving garden.

- **Water Wisely:** Always water at the base of plants to keep foliage dry and reduce fungal risks. Morning watering is best for allowing plants to dry off quickly.
- **Prune Regularly:** Remove damaged or diseased leaves to prevent issues from spreading. It also keeps foliage off the soil, where critters are waiting to feast.
- **Clean Your Tools:** Sanitize garden tools, especially after handling sick plants, to avoid spreading disease.

PHYSICAL BARRIERS

Some pests need an extra layer of defense.

- **Row Covers:** Lightweight, floating row covers protect crops like kale, broccoli, and cabbage from cabbage worms and beetles. They're incredibly effective but need to be applied as soon as the plants go in the ground to avoid trapping pests underneath.
- **Sticky Traps:** Yellow sticky traps are great for monitoring and controlling flying pests like aphids and whiteflies. They work wonders in greenhouses or small, enclosed gardens.
- **Copper Tape for Slugs:** Add copper tape around raised bed edges to deter slugs and snails. They can't stand the slight electric sensation it creates.

LAST RESORT TIPS

Sometimes, even the best-prepared gardener needs a backup plan.

- **DIY Pest Deterrents:** Garlic and chili sprays are natural, effective options. Blend garlic or chili peppers with water, strain, and spray onto leaves. This works surprisingly well against rabbits but needs frequent reapplication. (Note: The smell might not be ideal during pregnancy!)
- **Neem Oil:** This organic option disrupts pest life cycles while sparing beneficial insects. Apply it in the early morning or evening to avoid harming pollinators. Use sparingly-many gardeners rarely need it.

Recap of the Good Stuff!

- Permaculture focuses on interdependence among plants and minimizing waste.
- Organic gardening prioritizes eliminating chemicals and genetically modified seeds.
- By understanding plant relationships—such as beneficial pairings, competitive foes, and family connections—gardeners can design systems that promote biodiversity, minimize pests, and enhance soil health, resulting in a thriving, resilient garden.
- Perseverance is key: Gardening takes time, effort, and commitment, but the rewards are worth it!

Deep River Girls' Tea

Learn from the mistakes of others. You can't live long enough to make them all yourself.—Eleanor Roosevelt

Just Keep Swimming—*Dori, Finding Nemo*

YEAR ONE

The Foundation of Your Garden

Key for success—grow vegetables that are forgiving and simple to sow. Your first year will be full of challenges and learning curves. You are learning something new and that is amazing. Do you want the BEST results with veggies that produce and are not fussy? These crops are fast-growing and in many ways forgiving.

- Beans
- Peas
- Summer Squash
- Lettuce
- Spinach
- Marigolds
- Basil
- Tomatoes

These plants will boost your confidence. Once you get the hang of these, you'll be ready to tackle more challenging crops. In Year One, focus on mastering the basics and keeping things simple. Here's your checklist for success:

- **Choose Your Garden Site** – Pick the best spot for sunlight and accessibility.
- **Build Your Beds** – Raised beds or in-ground beds, depending on your space.
- **Keep Notes in Your 15-Minute Gardener Handbook** – Track everything from planting dates to watering schedules.
- **Learn About Seed Selection and Spacing** – Read this book and remember to start with 8-12 easy-to-grow varieties that you'll actually eat.
- **Understand Pest Protection and Companion Planting** – Build a natural defense system for your plants.
- **Learn About Watering and Weeding** – Water consistently and keep weeds under control.

- **Harvest and Preserve Your Bounty** – Learn how to store and preserve your crops for long-term use.
- **End-of-Season Garden Cleanup** – Tidy up your garden to avoid pests and prepare for next year.
- **Plan for Next Year** – Use your experience to plan bigger or different crops for Year Two.

Remember, gardening is a marathon, not a sprint. If you're like me, you might dream of running a full-fledged homestead—with a fermenting jar of something on the counter, a cow to milk, and an abundance of homegrown food. But burnout is real, and it's better to start small and succeed than to go big and get overwhelmed. Grow successfully in Year One, and it will snowball into Year Two and beyond.

Garden Thyme Checks

Sow Successful

- [ ] Revisit the Veggies We Eat and select a growing plan

- [ ] If you haven't tested your soil yet, it's a good idea to do that now!

- [ ] Test Your Tools: Check your watering can, hose, or irrigation setup. Does it work well? Fix any leaks or issues now.

- [ ] Plan for Success: Review seed catalogs. Look for varieties that are disease-resistant and noted to thrive in your particular weather challenges.

- [ ] Set realistic goals (that means start with a smaller garden this year)

- [ ] Celebrate small wins

VEGGIES WE EAT

Your Seed Ordering Cheat Sheet

Below is a chart for ordering your seeds. We've broken it down by plant family, so it's easier to make your selections. You can use the space in the box to note what variety you chose. I highly recommend that you look in the back of the book and pick a plan that has what you like to grow in it.

This may seem obvious, but—pick the veggies you eat. In your first year, your garden is your experiment. Stick with veggies you love or at least *want* to love. If you're not a huge veggie fan, start with the basics: carrots, onions, lettuce, tomatoes, cucumbers, and sweet peppers. There are usually enough ways to cook with those goodies that even the pickiest eaters will enjoy. The key is to start small and start basic. This is the key to maximizing time and actualizing the cash savings.

Recap:

1. Choose Your Seeds: Go through and select the plants you want to grow.
2. Pick a plan in the back that has most of what you like to grow.
3. Make notes for future years
4. *Advanced:* Check out the "Friends" and "Foes" columns. Planting with friends promotes growth, and avoiding foes keeps your plants happy. Go off plan by swapping veggies that work well together.
5. *Advanced:* The "Transplant vs Direct Sow" column tells you whether it's better to start indoors or plant straight in the ground.

Note: We've also included whether it's best to start these seeds from transplants, direct sow, or if either method works. I am a bit of a broken record on this point, but in the first year, I *highly* recommend starting with transplants and easy direct-sow varieties. Not only will this save time, seed starting is a skill all on its own and will be much more successful if you let it be a NEXT level skill.

Veggies We Eat

Plants	Family	Friends	Foes	Sow
Zinnias	Asteraceae	Beans, Corn, Cucumber	None known	Direct sow (Bold and easy to grow)
Wild Oregano	Lamiaceae	Peppers, Tomatoes	None known	Wild and wonderful
Tomatoes	Solanaceae	Basil, Onion, Marigold, Carrot	Cabbage, Corn, Potato	Transplant
Thyme	Lamiaceae	Cabbage, Beans, Carrot	None known	Transplant
Swiss Chard	Amaranthaceae	Onions, Cabbage, Beets	Spinach, Potatoes	Direct sow or Transplant
Sweet Peas	Fabaceae	Carrot, Radish, Turnips	None known	Direct sow
Sunflowers	Asteraceae	Beans, Cucumbers, Corn	Potato, Tomato	Direct sow (Big, bold, and beautiful)
Spinach	Amaranthaceae	Strawberries, Peas, Radishes	Potatoes, Chard	Direct sow (Quick and easy)
Shallots	Amaryllidaceae	Carrots, Beets, Lettuce	Peas, Beans	Transplant (bulbs) (or direct sow)
Rosemary	Lamiaceae	Beans, Cabbage, Carrot	None known	Transplant (Slow starter)

Veggies We Eat

Plant	Family	Friends (Companion Plants)	Foes (Avoid Planting Together)	Transplant / Direct Sow
Radish	Brassicaceae	Carrot, Cucumber, Lettuce	Hyssop, Turnip	Direct sow (They're speedy little guys)
Potatoes	Solanaceae	Calendula, Herbs, Cabbage	Tomatoes, Carrots, Onion	Direct sow (they like cool weather and take extra work)
Plant	Family	Friends (Companion Plants)	Foes (Avoid Planting Together)	Transplant / Direct Sow
Plant	Family	Friends (Companion Plants)	Foes (Avoid Planting Together)	Transplant / Direct Sow
Parsnip	Apiaceae	Peas, Lettuce, Cabbage	Carrot, Celery	Direct sow (Patient grower)
Oregano	Lamiaceae	Peppers, Tomatoes, Basil	None known	Transplant
Onions	Amaryllidaceae	Lettuce, Beets, Carrots	Peas, Beans	Transplant or Use bulbs(or direct sow)
Marigolds	Asteraceae	Beans, Tomatoes, Peppers	None known	Direct sow (Natural pest repellent)

Veggies We Eat

Lettuce	Asteraceae	Carrot, Onion, Cucumber	Celery, Parsnip, Garlic	Direct sow (Just sow and go!)
Lemon Balm	Lamiaceae	Oregano, Rosemary, Thyme	None known	Keep this in a pot
Leeks	Amaryllidaceae	Carrot, Celery, Beets	Beans	Transplant (or direct sow)
Lamb's Quarters	Amaranthaceae	Beans, Corn, Cucumbers	Peas	Direct sow (Wild and wonderful)
Kale	Brassicaceae	Peas, Beets, Carrot, Onion	Potato, Cabbage	Transplant (Or direct sow mark carefully because it is easy to weed seedlings)
Hot /Sweet Peppers	Solanaceae	Basil, Oregano, Onion	Fennel, Cabbage, Beans	Both (Transplant or direct sow)
Green Beans	Fabaceae	Cucumber, Radish, Sunflower	Tomatoes, Potatoes, Garlic (heavy feeder)	Both (Transplant or direct sow)
Gazania	Asteraceae	N/A	N/A	Direct sow (For hardy borders)

Veggies We Eat

Garlic	Amaryllidaceae	Beets, Carrots, Roses	Beans, Peas	Direct Sow
Fennel	Apiaceae	Coriander, Basil, Dill	Carrots, Parsnip, Celery	Direct sow (They like it their way)
Dill	Apiaceae	Cabbage, Onion, Lettuce	Carrots, Fennel	Direct sow (Quick grower)
Celery	Apiaceae	Leeks, Cabbage, Tomato	Parsnip, Carrot	Transplant (Needs a little help)
Cauliflower	Brassicaceae	Beets, Cabbage, Thyme	Tomatoes, Peppers	Transplant (Not too hot these guys like cooler temps)
Carrots	Apiaceae	Onion, Peas, Lettuce	Dill, Parsnip, Celery	Direct sow (put where they will not be disturbed)
Calypso Beans	Fabaceae	Corn, Sunflower	Tomatoes, Potatoes	Direct sow
Calendula	Asteraceae	Cabbage, Beets, Carrots	None known	Direct sow (For beauty & pollination)
Cabbage	Brassicaceae	Chamomile, Dill, Thyme, Beets	Strawberry, Tomato, Peas	Transplant (or direct sow)

Veggies We Eat

Broccoli	Brassicaceae	Beans, Beets, Cabbage	Tomato, Pepper, Corn	Transplant (Needs some love)
Beets	Amaranthaceae	Lettuce, Cabbage, Onion	Pole Beans, Spinach	Direct sow or transplant (They don't mind either)
Basil	Lamiaceae	Tomato, Pepper, Lettuce, Oregano	Rue, Sage, Fennel	Transplant (A little pampering goes a long way)
Amaranth	Amaranthaceae	Beans, Peas, Okra	Carrots, Cabbage	Direct sow (Pretty independent)

Deep River Girl's Tea Thyme

Teach your kids what hot peppers look and taste like.

Spicy surprises are not much fun. We had a little guy

eat a habanero thinking it was sweet!

End of Harvest

Looking to the Next Seasons

PRESERVING THE SEASON

Recipes and Tips for Keeping Your Harvest

END OF SEASON

How to clean up well to set you up for growing success.

YEAR TWO, THREE AND BEYOND

Planning for growth.

While the earth remains, seedtime and harvest, cold and heat, summer and winter, day and night, shall not cease. Genesis 8:22 ESV

HARVEST AND ENDING WELL

There is nothing more cyclical than seasons. With that said, harvest is hardly the end. It is the beginning of so many things, not the least of which is celebration. **You are a gardener.**

Congratulations. Look at all the abundance you grew!

Before we jump into the vegetable descriptions, I want to wrap up our growth phase by giving a brief overview of the end of season work.

We talk about more of the *specifics* of harvest in the next section as we look at each individual plant.

Harvest is a task that is full of excitement in the beginning but can become monotonous as the months go on. Hopefully it never gets old. If you are finding that life happens and you have plants getting overripe, remember to remove these fruits. Rotting fruits attract pests and problems for your garden as a whole. But after you have eaten and shared the harvest, what do you do with the REST?

Preserving the harvest

Flowers are hung upside down to dry, onions are braided and hung in a cool garage, and potatoes are dug and stored out of the light of the sun. There are some veggies that are super easy to preserve because it simply means storing them in optimal conditions. Garlic for a year is really not hard to grow and it is crazy easy to keep. But what do we do with items like tomatoes, peppers or beets that are more complicated to store?

Canning, fermenting and dehydration are my go-to methods for preserving. These topics are fascinating and nuanced enough to each be their own book. For your first year, I suggest letting the freezer be your friend. Freeze as much of your extra goodies as you can. This works well with spinach, kale, tomatoes, carrots, herbs, and zucchini. And green beans, peas, broccoli. Peppers don't love being frozen, but there are ways to do it well. Blanching—quickly dipping in boiling water and then cooling in ice water before freezing—helps preserve some crispness.

I both pressure can and water bath can. Because these methods are an investment upfront and time consuming, I don't consider them "15 Minute Friendly". We do our canning in what I refer to as the "cracks of time". I rarely have a whole day to set aside for canning. We also can over 500 jars a year. So canning happens as we have a moment a couple of times a week. You will find canning supplies **available/not available** perpetually from August to October. I will make the sauce one day while we do school or during a nap time and run the canners the next day. It's the same principle—I give canning what I have when it fits in our schedule. I stay consistent though, and just like the garden—it works.

My favorite way to preserve, because of the health benefits, is ferments. I love fermenting beets, carrots, cabbage, and even zucchini pickle that is delicious. We eat ferments almost daily during the winter. It is amazing for the gut balance and even our kids love them. My husband hated pickles but as we switched our diet his taste buds changed and he loves a good ferment now too.

End-of-Season Cleanup

We celebrate all year with food we have grown. Here are a couple of recipes to help you savor your harvest. Don't skip the reflection pages and checklists at the end! Make a few notes for your older self and future generations. They will love you the more for it. Trust me.

Salty Garlic Sauerkraut

INGREDIENTS

- 1 medium head of cabbage (about 2–3 lbs)
- 1 ½ tablespoons salt (non-iodized, like sea salt or pickling salt)
- 2–3 garlic cloves, minced or sliced

½ teaspoon caraway seeds (optional, for classic kraut flavor)

If mold forms on top, scrape it off—it's harmless.

If the kraut smells off or slimy, toss it and try again.

The longer it ferments, the tangier it gets!

Enjoy your homemade garlic sauerkraut on sandwiches, sausages, or straight from the jar!

DIRECTIONS

- Prep the Cabbage
- Remove the outer leaves and set one aside.
- Slice the cabbage into thin shreds.
- Massage with Salt
- Place cabbage in a large bowl, sprinkle salt over it, and start massaging.
- Do this for about 5–10 minutes until it softens and releases liquid (brine).
- Add Garlic & Pack the Jar
- Mix in the garlic (and caraway if using).
- Pack the cabbage tightly into a clean ½-gallon glass jar, pressing down as you go.
- Pour the brine from the bowl over the cabbage until fully submerged.
- Weigh it Down
- Use the reserved outer cabbage leaf to cover the shredded cabbage, tucking it down.
- Place a fermentation weight or a small jar filled with water on top to keep everything under the brine.
- Cover & Ferment
- Loosely cover the jar with a lid or a cloth secured with a rubber band.
- Let it ferment at room temperature (65-75°F) for 1-3 weeks. Check daily to ensure cabbage stays submerged.
- Taste & Store

Start tasting after a week. Once it's tangy enough for you, remove the weight, seal the jar, and store it in the fridge for up to 6 months.

Summer Pasta with Garlic & Basil

INGREDIENTS

- 1 lb pasta (any type, or use zucchini noodles for a low-carb option)
- 2 tbsp olive oil
- 4 garlic cloves, pressed or minced
- 2 tomatoes, chopped
- 1/4 cup fresh basil, chopped
- 1/2 cup feta, crumbled
- 1 bell pepper, finely chopped

DIRECTIONS

- Cook the pasta according to package directions. Drain and set aside.
- Sauté the veggies – In a large pan, heat olive oil over medium heat. Add garlic and cook for 30 seconds until fragrant. Toss in tomatoes and peppers, cooking until soft (about 3–4 minutes).
- Combine – Add the sautéed veggies to the cooked pasta and toss well.
- Top it off – Stir in fresh basil and crumbled feta. Adjust seasoning with salt & pepper.
- Bonus: Serve with gyro-style meatballs for extra protein and flavor!
- Serving Tip: Pair with a simple side salad or garlic bread for a full meal.
- Make it Spicy: Add red pepper flakes or a drizzle of chili oil!
- Enjoy your Summer Pasta—quick, delicious, and packed with fresh flavors!
-

Beet and Bacon Salad

INGREDIENTS

- Mixed greens (spinach, arugula, or romaine—your choice!)
- 1/2 red onion, thinly sliced
- 6 slices of bacon (or turkey bacon, if you must!)
- 2 medium beets, peeled & diced
- 1/4 cup goat cheese, crumbled
- 2 tbsp balsamic vinegar
- 1 tbsp olive oil
    - 1 tsp honey (optional, for a hint of sweetness)
    - Salt & pepper to taste

The crispy, salty bite of bacon pairs perfectly with the sweet, roasted beets and creamy goat cheese. And let's be honest, anything deglazed with balsamic vinegar is going to taste amazing.

DIRECTIONS

- Prep the veggies – Wash, chop, and get everything ready.
- Sauté the onions & bacon – In a pan over medium heat, cook the bacon and onions together until the onions are caramelized and the bacon is crispy.
- Add the beets – When the bacon is halfway done, toss in the diced beets and let them cook in the bacon drippings until tender.
- Make the dressing – Deglaze the pan with balsamic vinegar, scraping up all the flavorful bits. Add olive oil, honey (if using), and a pinch of salt & pepper. Stir well.
- Assemble the salad – Toss the greens with the warm bacon-beet mixture. Sprinkle with goat cheese and drizzle with the balsamic dressing.
- Serve immediately – Enjoy warm or at room temp for maximum flavor!
- Pro Tip: For extra crunch, add toasted walnuts or sunflower seeds.
- Enjoy your Beet & Bacon Salad—where earthy meets smoky in the best way!

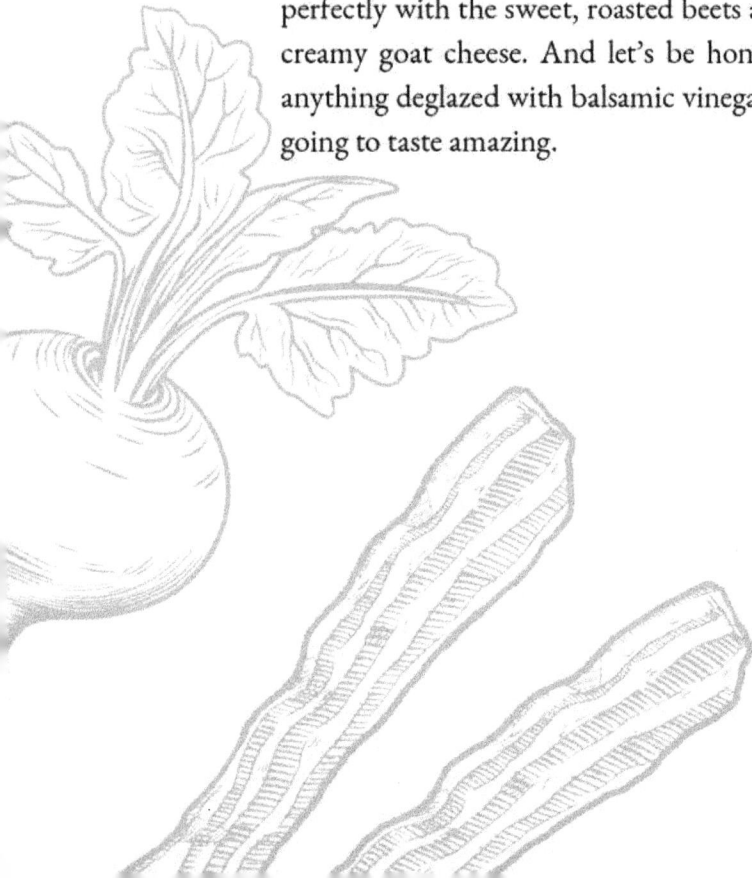

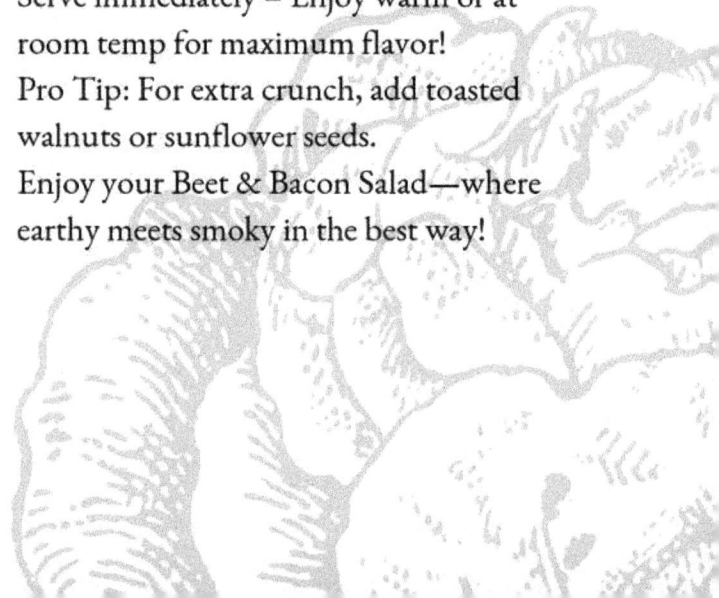

Garden Clean-Up
15 Minutes Checklist

30-Day Garden Cleanup Schedule. Begin 2-3 weeks after the last frost but can be delayed even longer as weather permits. I like to do this in December.

WEEK 1

- ✓ Remove dead plants, and sort them for compost vs. trash
- ✓ Collect and label seeds from healthy plants
- ✓ Clean and sanitize all garden tools
- ✓ Test soil pH in each bed
- ✓ Take "end of season" photos for records
- ✓ Inventory remaining seeds and supplies

WEEK 2

- ✓ Remove tomato cages, stakes, store clean
- ✓ Roll up and store hoses (x 2)
- ✓ Remove any diseased plant material (x2)
- ✓ Freeze Herbs for winter
- ✓ Start a compost pile with healthy debris
- ✓ Make sure tools are put away and don't overwinter in the garden.

WEEK 3

- ✓ . Add 2" compost to each bed
- ✓ Top beds with **shredded** leaves
- ✓ Mulch perennial herbs heavily
- ✓ Clean and store containers
- ✓ Weekend project: Organize garden shed/garage. Technically if I "cleaned up as I went" this would not be such a big task. But cut yourself a break you grew a garden this year!

WEEK 4

- ✓ Cover beds with cardboard/thick mulch
- ✓ Store garden amendments properly
- ✓ Final site cleanup and tool check
- ✓ Review Garden Notes.
- ✓ Make garden plan for next year.
- ✓ Label seeds, stored containers etc. cleatrly for spring.

Looking Ahead
Year 2 & 3 and Beyond

A Quick Overview

••

YEAR TWO: EXPANDING YOUR SKILLS AND GARDEN

By Year Two, you'll have a better understanding of your garden's needs. It's time to experiment a bit more and challenge yourself:

✓ Expand Your Garden – If you're ready, add two more raised beds to give yourself more growing space. You should be able to manage up to 6 beds in 15 minutes a day.

✓ Try 2 New Veggie Varieties: like carrots, beets, or potatoes.

✓ Try Starting Flowers. Zinnias and marigolds are easy to start, cost-effective, and will brighten your garden.

✓ Add Fertilizer – Learn how to nourish your soil with balanced fertilizers to improve crop yields—if you didn't get to it year one start that worm farm.

✓ Plan a Late-Fall Garden – Extend your harvest season with cool-weather crops like kale or root vegetables.

✓ Learn how to use a Dehydrator and Water Bath Canner.

YEAR THREE: ROOTED

You've grown more than food—now you're growing systems. Year Three is about deepening your relationship with your garden and turning it into a more productive and efficient space.

Expand or Diversify Your Garden Layout
Try starting seeds, adding more vertical spaces, or a perennial border. You don't have to go bigger—just smarter.

Add Perennials
Include asparagus, rhubarb, strawberries, or herbs like oregano and thyme that return each year

Invite Beneficial Insects
Plant yarrow, alyssum, or dill to attract pollinators and predators like ladybugs. Learn to recognize friend vs. foe insects!

Save Seeds from Your Best Plants
Start small with easy-to-save seeds like beans, peas, or tomatoes. Label and store them for next year.

Preserve the Harvest
Build on your water bath canning skills and learn pressure canning. Explore fermentation (like pickles or sauerkraut) or vacuum sealing for freezer storage.

Test and Amend Soil Based on Results
Order a soil test and learn how to interpret the results. Amend accordingly with compost, lime, or specific nutrients.

Reflection and Future

Planning Chart

Easy 15-Minute Tasks to Keep You Tidy Until Spring

As the gardening season winds down, I like to take my time with fall cleanup, starting at the end of October and easing into December. Partially because I like to savor the process and partially because I get tired. One of the most common questions I get is how I manage to get so much done. The secret? I just keep going. If I don't finish a 30-day plan in 30 days, that's okay—it's more important to finish. I hope this mindset helps you feel relaxed about the process and gives you the freedom to work at your own pace.

Reflection	Your Thoughts	Future Goals
What brought you the most joy?		
What challenges did you overcome?		
What new goals will you set for next year?		

I trust in nature for the stable laws of beauty and utility.
Spring shall plant and autumn garner to the end of
time." — Robert Browning

Notes

Planning for the Future

Garden Thyme Checks

Ending Well

End-of-Season Cleanup
We celebrate all year with food we have grown. Here are a couple of recipes to help you savor your harvest. Don't skip the reflection pages. Make a few notes for your older self. You will love yourself the more for it. Trust me.

☐ **Review Phases**—What do you have left to complete? Make sure you revisit the topic below.

☐ **Track Notes** – Record planting dates, watering schedules, and any lessons learned in your 15-Minute Gardener Handbook.

☐ **Learn Pest Protection** – Research companion planting and natural pest deterrents.

☐ **Start a Compost Pile** – Begin turning garden waste into organic matter for next season.

☐ **Water Consistently** – Develop a simple watering routine for consistent care.
☐ **Weed Regularly** – Stay on top of weeds for healthy, thriving plants.
☐ **Harvest & Preserve** – Learn basic harvesting and storage techniques for your crops.

☐ **End-of-Season Cleanup** – Make a note on your calendar—when will you begin?
Plan for Next Year – Reflect on what worked well and plan for bigger or different crops.

"Then our sons in their youth will be like well-nurtured plants, and our daughters will be like pillars carved to adorn a palace. Our barns will be filled with every kind of provision. Our sheep will increase by thousands, by tens of thousands in our fields; our oxen will draw heavy loads. There will be no breaching of walls, no going into captivity, no cry of distress in our streets. Blessed is the people of whom this is true; blessed is the people whose God is the LORD."
Psalm144:12-15 NIV 1995

It's exciting to see things coming up again, plants that you've had twenty or thirty years.
It's like seeing an old friend." — Tasha Tudor

Part 2: Plant Families

Think of this section as the best friend that you can go to any time for tips about a specific plant. It will also give you the information you need so that you can follow the planting plans with confidence. If you are passionate about plants then this section is for you. But if you just want the 15-minute shortcut—just read about the members you are planning to plant this year. This will keep you focused and out of overwhelm. Save the study for winter and quieter days.

"Don't judge each day by the harvest you reap but by the seeds that you plant." — Robert Louis Stevenson

Stop hauling water (Don't waste time). -Joel Salatin

Be Loved. Sow Love. Grow Family.

Deep River Gardens Family Motto

Amaranth

Beets

Amaranthaceae

A Colorful Bounty

Spinach

Swiss Chard

AMARANTHACEAE

Super Food Family

Plant family names like "Amaranthaceae" can definitely feel like a mouthful and when I first encountered them, I thought, "Do I really need to bother with this? Can't I just plant seeds and skip the science part?" The short answer is, yes—you *can* plant seeds without diving into the science. But the long answer? Understanding plant families opens up a whole new level of gardening mastery.

Think of it like meeting a new friend with a name you can't quite pronounce. Sure, you might struggle at first, but once you get it, you start to see the connections—how their family dynamics shape who they are and how they interact with the world. The same goes for plants. By learning a plant's "last name," you unlock clues about how it grows, what it needs to thrive, and what might hurt it.

Understanding plant families isn't just a bonus—it's a key to making your garden flourish. So let's dive into the science and spark your curiosity. We'll make sense of these names together, and I promise, by the end of it, you'll see how this knowledge transforms your garden from average to thriving.

Plant Families are like a garden version of your family tree. Spinach and Swiss chard are siblings with shared traits, needs, and vulnerabilities. Understanding these connections makes your garden more intuitive and successful.

The Amaranthaceae family is the garden's secret powerhouse, boasting versatile champions like amaranth, spinach, and Swiss chard. These plants are tough, adaptable, and drought-tolerant, thriving in a range of conditions while delivering stunning foliage and nutrient-packed greens. Think of them as the cool, confident all-rounders who bring beauty and productivity to your garden.

Friends: The Garden Allies

Pair Amaranthaceae plants with beans, carrots, and cucumbers for a harmonious garden. Beans enrich the soil with nitrogen, while cucumbers and carrots provide shade and support. Together, they create a balanced ecosystem where everyone thrives.

Foes: The Nutrient Competitors

Every garden has conflicts; for these Super Greens, it's Brassicas (like cabbage, broccoli, and kale). These two groups compete for the same nutrients, making them less than ideal bedmates. Keep them separated in your garden plan and everyone will thrive.

Soil: The Foundation of Success

Amaranthaceae plants flourish in fertile, well-draining soil packed with organic matter. Since these greens absorb nutrients directly into their leaves, the quality of your soil is key. Prep your bed with compost and ensure any added manure is well-composted and buried beneath the topsoil.

Pro Tip:

If your soil is underwhelming, side-dress with compost mid-season to give your greens a boost. Happy soil equals vibrant, delicious harvests!

Size: From Subtle to Showstopper

This family offers options for every garden space. Swiss chard and spinach are compact and perfect for borders or interplanting while towering amaranth adds drama and height to any garden bed. They're like the tall friend who knows how to make an entrance!

Temperature & Light: Mixed

These sun-loving plants thrive best with plenty of light. Spinach prefers cooler temperatures, thriving between 50°F (10°C) and 75°F (24°C), making it perfect for spring and fall. Amaranth, a true heat lover, soars in temperatures above 70°F (21°C), making it the star of summer gardens.

Watering: Steady and Balanced

While Amaranthaceae plants can handle dry spells once established, they do need consistent moisture early on. Keep the soil evenly moist during germination and young growth but avoid waterlogging.
Think of it like a refreshing mist, not a torrential downpour.

Pests & Diseases:

Leaf Munchers

The main troublemakers for Amaranthaceae plants are the bugs that eat the leaves- the precious crop of most varieties in this family.

Leaf-munching pests are the top offenders—aphids, leaf miners, and flea beetles all love this family.

> *Flea beetles* = cosmetic damage

> *Aphids* = full-on eradication if ignored

Diseases like downy mildew and leaf spot show up in damp conditions.

What to do:

> Space plants well to improve airflow

> Plant companions that attract beneficial bugs

> Blast pests off with a strong hose spray (do it regularly)

> Dip leaves in soapy water to manage infestations

> Pull problem plants without guilt—these grow fast and bounce back

Bottom line: Prevention is everything. Don't let one bad leaf ruin the bunch.

Fun Fact: Superfood

Amaranth seeds are an ancient superfood, packed with protein and prized by the Aztecs. Their stunning red foliage also makes them a favorite for ornamental gardens—a practical and beautiful choice!

Pro Tip: Sweet Frost-Kissed Greens

A light frost can sweeten greens like Swiss chard and spinach, giving them a richer flavor and extending your harvest season. Cold weather isn't the enemy for these hardy plants—it's an ally!

Amaranthaceae plants are multitaskers that deliver resilience, beauty, and nutrition to any garden. Care for them well, and they'll reward you with a vibrant, thriving plot.

Now, let's meet the members!

Beets

Difficulty Level: Easy

Best For: Beginners, root vegetable enthusiasts, and vibrant garden displays. We LOVE beets. Rich in anthocyanins—these are traditionally considered a "blood cleansing" vegetable. Their deep tap roots mean they draw trace minerals from deep in the soil. If you've only tried a pickled beet at a buffet, consider trying them roasted with potatoes and carrots in a stew. Or sautéed with bacon (so good).

Favorite Varieties

- **Detroit Red:** Classic red beet is known for its sweet flavor and smooth texture.
- **Candy Stripe (Chioggia):** Striking red-and-white rings inside, though it can be less sweet with a slight earthy tang.
- **Golden:** Bright yellow roots with a milder, slightly nutty taste. Note: These colorful varieties may not be as sweet due to geosmin—an organic compound found in all beets.

Growing Guide

- **Birthday:** 5-10 days after planting.
- **Days to Maturity:** 50–70 days
- **When to Start:** Early spring or late summer for fall harvest
- **Special Spacing Requirements:** Thin seedlings to 3–4 inches apart once they're a few inches tall to give roots space to develop.

Harvesting

- **When to Harvest:** when roots are 1.5–3 inches in diameter for best flavor.
- **How to Harvest and Store:** Loosen the soil around the base and gently pull the beets out by their tops. The sweetest beets are small and have naturally lower levels of geosim.
- **Storage Tips:** Scrub beets well. This is one veggie I recommend peeling for the sweetest flavor. Trim greens to 1 inch above the root, then store in a cool, humid place for 1–3 months.

Pro Tips & Quirks

- Avoid letting beets grow too large—they can become woody and lose flavor.
- Thin beets: Seed pods hold many seeds, so make sure to thin for ideal development.
- Fun fact: The greens are a superfood in their own right—don't toss! Wash and throw them into a pan and sauté like spinach, or toss into a protein-banana smoothie, and not even the kids will complain.

Swiss Chard

Difficulty Level: Easy

Best For: Colorful gardens, edible landscaping, and frequent harvesting.

Favorite Variety

- **Rainbow Chard:** A mix of bright stems (red, yellow, pink, orange) that add a burst of color and mild flavor to dishes.

Growing Guide

- **Birthday:** around 10 days after planting
- **Days to Maturity:** 50–60 days for mature leaves; baby greens in 30 days.
- **When to Start:** Early spring or late summer for a fall crop.
- **Special Spacing Requirements:** Space plants 6–12 inches apart to allow ample room for leaf production.

Harvesting

- **When to Harvest:** Start harvesting outer leaves when they're 6–8 inches long; leave the inner ones to keep growing.
- **How to Harvest:** Cut leaves near the base using scissors or a sharp knife.
- **Storage Tips:** Keep unwashed leaves in a plastic bag in the fridge for up to a week.

Pro Tips & Quirks

- Pro Tip: Swiss chard is incredibly frost-tolerant and can even survive light snow!
- Unique Characteristic: Unlike spinach, Swiss chard doesn't bolt as quickly in the heat, making it a reliable summer green.
- Fun fact: Like the beet seed, the swiss chard seed is actually several seeds in one!

Friends: Beets love onions, chives and garlic, they also pair well with lettuce, herbs and bush beans.

Foes: Beets are sensitive to fennel and can compete with the heavy feeders in the garden like brassicas and pole beans.

Spinach

Difficulty Level: Easy

Best For: Cool-season gardening and quick, nutritious harvests. Like most greens, spinach does not like heat. If you are reaching above 90°F, plan on planting in partial shade or saving for early and late season. Make sure to keep watered. Drying out causes greens to get bitter.

Favorite Varieties

- **Winter Bloomsdale:** A cold-hardy variety with crinkled, flavorful leaves.
- **Tyee:** A heat-tolerant summer spinach with smooth, tender leaves.

Growing Guide:

- **Birthday:** about 7 days after planting.
- **Days to Maturity:** 35–50 days
- **When to Start:** Early spring or late summer for fall crops; winter varieties can be grown in mild climates.
- **Special Spacing Requirements:** Space 3–6 inches apart to encourage proper airflow and reduce disease risk.

Harvesting:

- **When to Harvest:** Harvest baby leaves at 3 inches or mature leaves at 6 inches.
- **How to Harvest:** Pinch or cut individual leaves; for a larger harvest, cut the plant at the base, leaving 1 inch to regrow.
- **Storage Tips:** Store unwashed leaves in a sealed bag in the fridge for up to a week.

Pro Tips & Quirks

- Pro Tip: Plant spinach in partial shade during warmer months to extend the harvest.
- **Common Mistake:** Don't let spinach bolt—once it starts flowering, the leaves turn bitter.

Friends: Spinach pairs well with everything. Shade tolerant and cool loving.

Foes: Spinach is a versitile favorite with few enemies. Just keep it well fed.

Amaranth

Difficulty Level: Moderate

Best For: Small Spaces, Pollinator-Friendly Gardens, Ornamental Appeal

Favorite Varieties:

- **Burgundy:** Tall, striking red foliage that doubles as an edible and ornamental plant.
- **Golden Giant:** A variety known for its vibrant golden seed heads and impressive height.

Growing Guide

- **Birthday:** about 7-10 days from seed.
- **Days to Maturity:** 60-75 days for greens; 90-120 days for seeds.
- **When to Start:** Direct sow after the last frost date when soil temperatures consistently stay above 70°F (21°C).
- **Special Spacing Requirements:** Space plants 12-18 inches apart to allow ample room for their tall, leafy growth.
- **Light Requirements:** Full sun for optimal growth.

Special Care Notes

- Amaranth is drought-tolerant but benefits from consistent watering during germination and early growth. Avoid overwatering to prevent root issues.
- This is also an impressive beauty in the garden. Grow for the 'wow' factor.

Harvesting:

- **When to Harvest:** Harvest young leaves when they're tender, usually 30-40 days after planting. Seeds are ready when the flower heads dry out and seeds loosen easily.
- **How to Harvest:** Cut leaves as needed or snip seed heads and shake them in a paper bag to collect seeds.
- **Storage Tips:** Store seeds in a cool, dry place. Leaves are best used fresh but can be refrigerated for up to a week.

Pro Tips & Quirks

- Plant amaranth alongside vibrant pollinator-friendly plants like zinnias or marigolds for a stunning garden centerpiece.

- Interplant with fast-growing greens (like rainbow chard or lettuce) to maximize bed usage while waiting for amaranth to mature.
- Amaranth can self-seed if left unchecked, so harvest seeds promptly to prevent unwanted volunteers.

Friends: Rainbow chard, kale, and other bright greens make a stunning visual combination. Pair with zinnias or marigolds to attract pollinators.

Foes: Avoid planting near heavy nitrogen-feeders like Brassicas to prevent competition for nutrients.

Wild to Wonderful

Lamb's Quarters

Lamb's Quarters *(Chenopodium album)*
Often overlooked as a common weed, lamb's quarters are a nutrient-packed gem of the Amaranthaceae family. Historically popular before spinach took center stage, these wild greens are true superfoods. These greens also benefit from a strong taproot that pulls up essential minerals from deep within the soil, enriching their leaves with unparalleled nutrients.

Slicer
Tomato

Cherry
Tomato

Hot Pepper

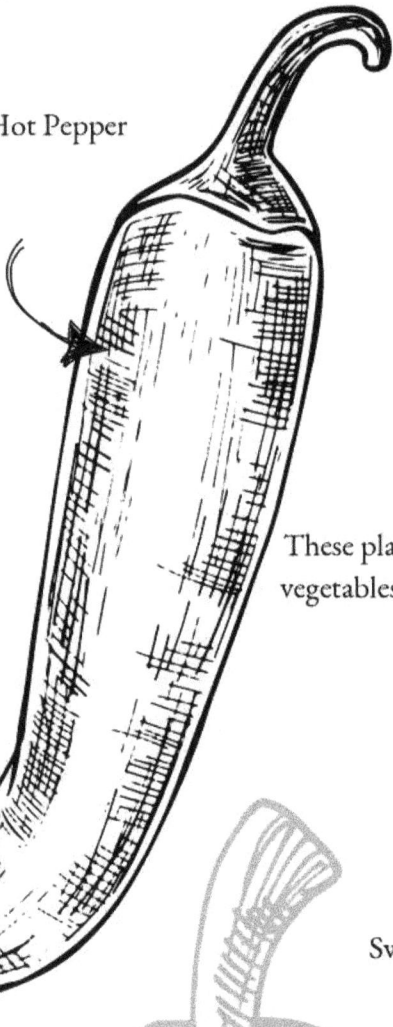

Solanaceae

Solanaceae Family

These plants are sun-loving and versatile, producing some of the most beloved vegetables and fruits in the garden. With the right care, they'll reward you with bountiful harvests of flavorful produce.

EggPlant

Sweet Pepper

Potato

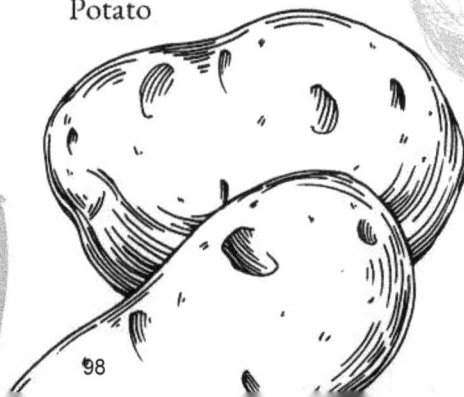

98

SOLANACEAE

Lovers of Sun Family

The **Solanaceae family,** also known as the Nightshade family, is home to some of the most beloved garden vegetables and fruits. Think tomatoes, peppers, potatoes, and eggplants—these plants are versatile, flavorful, and incredibly rewarding when given the right care. Whether you're a seasoned gardener or a newcomer to growing your food, this family is one you'll want to know well.

Growing Conditions Specific to This Family

Solanaceae plants are all about sun and warmth. They thrive in rich, well-drained soil with plenty of organic matter, so amend the soil with compost or aged manure before planting to give them the nutrients they need. These plants prefer slightly acidic soil, with a pH ranging from 6.0 to 6.8. Since they are heat lovers, don't rush to plant them too early—wait until the danger of frost has well passed, and the soil has warmed up to about 60°F (16°C). Potatoes are the exception and tolerate cooler temperatures and even a light frost without a problem. Tomatoes and peppers like their roots warm and they don't appreciate cold feet! This is a high nutrient-demand family. Be generous with your compost and amendments before planting.

Common Family Traits

- Heat-loving, full-sun enthusiasts: They love basking in the sun, soaking up those warm rays to fuel their growth and fruit production.
- Thrive in nutrient-rich, slightly acidic soils: They are not picky, but they do prefer a rich environment to grow in.
- Medium to tall growers: Solanaceae plants are often the towering stars of the garden,
- Require consistent moisture but well-drained conditions: Keep the soil evenly moist, but don't let it sit in soggy conditions—they need well-drained soil to prevent root rot.

Friends

- **Basil, parsley, carrots, and onions** are excellent companions for Solanaceae plants. Basil, in particular, loves to grow alongside tomatoes, helping to deter pests like aphids and improving the overall flavor of your tomatoes. Parsley can act as a natural pest repellent as well. Carrots and onions help with soil health and will happily share garden space without causing any drama

Foes

- **Brassicas** (like cabbage and broccoli) and **fennel** should be avoided nearby. These plants can compete for similar nutrients, leaving your Solanaceae plants feeling neglected. Fennel, in particular, tends to release chemicals that can inhibit the growth of nearby plants. Not a good neighbor in the garden!

Pests and Diseases

- Watch out for **aphids, whiteflies, and hornworms.** Aphids can be sneaky little pests, sucking away the juices from your plants. Whiteflies love to infest the undersides of leaves, while hornworms can completely defoliate your plants in a matter of days. A quick sweep through your garden daily can help keep these troublemakers in check.
- **Frequent Diseases:** Blight is the nightmare of tomatoes, and **blossom end rot** can cause you to lose perfectly good fruits. The key to preventing these issues is crop rotation (don't plant your Solanaceae family members in the same spot year after year) and avoiding overhead watering. Water at the base of the plants to keep the leaves dry, and you'll reduce the risk of many common diseases.

Hot Peppers

Difficulty Level: Moderate

Best For: Small Space, Spice Lovers (who can handle the heat!)

Favorite Varieties

- **Jalapeno:** The classic go-to for fresh salsas and poppin' heat. If you want to keep things mild to medium, these are your peppers.
- **Habanero:** These little guys are like the fiery heart of a dragon. Seriously hot—perfect for those who want to feel the burn.
- **Cayenne:** Great for homemade cayenne pepper. Want to spice up your life and your food? These will do it.
- **Serrano:** A bit milder than the habanero but still packing a punch. Great for pickling or tossing into a stir fry!
- **Thai Bird's Eye:** These tiny peppers are the spice kings of Southeast Asia. When they say, "small but mighty", they aren't kidding.

Growing Guide:

- **Birthday:** about 25 days from seed.
- **Days to Maturity:** 75-90 days (They don't rush, they just make you wait for all that fiery goodness.)
- **When to Start:** Let's be real: Starting from seeds is super economical but you know what is *more* fun? Transplants. Yep, buying those babies as little plants is a lot easier and less stressful. Trust me, no one needs a mini greenhouse disaster in their living room.
- **Special Spacing Requirements:** Space them about 12 inches apart, so they don't get too cozy and start crowding each other out.
- **Light Requirements:** Full sun

Special Care Notes

- Keep them warm. These are great ones to put last on your planting cycle. Like your cucurbits, they don't like to get chilled.
- Don't drown them with water. Keep things balanced, and they'll be happy.
- Fertilize with a low-nitrogen fertilizer. Think of it as their spa treatment to keep them strong without too much "fluff."

Harvesting

- **When to Harvest:** Wait until they're fully ripe (usually bright red, orange, or yellow). The longer they sit, the hotter they get. It's like they're saving up all their spice power just for you.
- **How to Harvest:** Scissors or pruning shears, because no one has time to rip peppers off the plant like a savage.
- **Storage tips:** Dry 'em out, or pop them in an airtight container. Want to make cayenne pepper? Just grind those bad boys up and enjoy the burn.

Pro Tips & Quirks

- Transplants are a godsend. I get it, you want to start from seed because you're frugal, but trust me: *buying* your peppers as transplants will save you frustration, time, and sanity.
- Be careful when handling these little heat grenades. Wear gloves! That burning sensation on your hands will make you regret everything when you accidentally rub your eyes.
- Hot peppers are the spice version of a reality show. You never really know how hot they are until they hit your mouth, and even then, it's a *wild* ride.
- Do NOT add nitrogen-rich fertilizer or compost to these plants.

Friends: If you're looking for perfect pairings, try planting peppers alongside basil or onions for some flavor fiesta. Nastriums and Marigolds look fantastic nearby.

Foes: Stay away from beans and peas. *Here's the deal*—Peppers and beans/peas don't always get along because of something called nitrogen fixation. Beans and peas are part of the legume family, and they have a special power: they can pull nitrogen out of the air and put it into the soil. Sounds like a superpower, right? Well, here's the catch: peppers (and other nightshades) *don't love* too much nitrogen. While nitrogen is essential for plant growth, too much of it can lead to lush, leafy plants that produce fewer fruits (peppers, in this case). So, when beans and peas are too close to peppers, they can throw off the nitrogen balance, leading to less productive pepper plants. In a 4x8 bed, I have found that planting at opposite sides of the box is usually far enough away. If you notice reduced production, make a note and separate the next planting.

Tomatoes

Difficulty Level: Moderate
Best For: Medium to Large Spaces, Intermediate Gardeners

Tomatoes are a staple in the garden—and for good reason. With varieties ranging from sweet cherry tomatoes, succulent slicers, to thick-walled canning types, there's something for every gardener.
Whether you're after the perfect sandwich slice or a rich, meaty sauce, tomatoes are a versatile favorite. When I grow, I grow for flavor and color so you'll see a variety of both in my favorite picks (I refuse to *only* plant red tomatoes!). Tomatoes come in three major categories:

- **Cherry Tomatoes:** Typically indeterminate. *(Indeterminate tomatoes continue to grow and produce fruit throughout the growing season.)* These bite-sized bursts of sweetness are perfect for salads, snacking, or tossing into a pasta dish. They grow vigorously and produce heavily, so make sure you've got a sturdy trellis or cage to support them.
- **Slicer Tomatoes:** Typically indeterminate. The classic tomato, perfect for sandwiches or eating fresh. These larger varieties require more room to grow so be sure to give them adequate space in your garden and support them with strong cages.
- **Canner Tomatoes:** If you're into canning, these are the tomatoes for you. Dense and meaty, they're

ideal for sauces, soups, and preserving. Keep them well-watered during the growing season for a bountiful harvest. These are most often determinate, meaning they fruit heavily all at once, making them ideal for large batch processing.

Tomato Varieties

- **Mountain Merit**
  - *Determinate, medium size.*
  - Reliable with a balanced flavor and excellent disease resistance. Great for fresh eating and slicing.

- **Brandywine Red**
  - *Indeterminate, large size.*
  - A classic heirloom with a juicy, sweet flavor. Perfect for sandwiches and fresh eating.

- **Cherokee Carbon**
  - *Indeterminate, medium-large size.*
  - Deep red with a rich, smoky flavor. These manageable vines are great for smaller gardens or trellised spaces. Excellent for fresh eating or slicing.

- **Gin Fizz**
  - *Indeterminate, medium size.*
  - Stunning yellow and pink tomatoes with a light, fresh flavor. Beautiful addition to salads or as a colorful garnish.

- **Roma Types (San Marzano & Grandera)**
  - *Determinate, medium size.*
  - Known for their dense, meaty texture, these tomatoes are ideal for sauce-making, canning, and soups.

Growing Guide

- Birthday: 7-14 days from seed
- Days to Maturity: 60-85 days
- When to Start: 6-8 weeks before the last frost indoors
- Special Spacing: 18-24 inches apart
- Light Requirements: Full sun (6-8 hours minimum)

Special Care Notes

- Base watering only to prevent disease, keep leaves dry
- Reduce nitrogen after the initial growth phase to focus energy on fruit production
- Temperature sensitive-protect from frost with row covers or by starting later in the season
- Requires sturdy trellising support-use a cattle panel for 4x8 raised beds

Harvesting

- When to Harvest: With colored varieties, harvest when the tomato is still firm and color is vibrant.
- Method: Twist gently or cut with small clippers.
- Storage: Room temperature only, never refrigerate
- Preservation: Suitable for canning or freezing. Any tomato can be canned but other varieties have more seeds which is generally frowned on for sauces. On the other hand, the flavor and surprise of a yellow sauce *is* delightful.

Pro Tips & Quirks

- Cattle panel trellis is the best choice for 4x8 raised beds (it creates a sturdy arch and saves space)
- F1 hybrids offer disease resistance and specific traits (and they're not GMO!)
- Transplants are the way to go for beginners to save you time and frustration!
- Proper spacing is crucial for air circulation—crowding leads to disease
- Determinate vs. Indeterminate:
  - Determinate: Bush-type, compact growth; good for container gardens and small spaces. You can put a stake in the ground and call it done.
  - Indeterminate: Vining types, continuous growth; perfect for larger gardens and trellising.

Friends: Basil, onions, carrots, lettuc, zinnias, marigolds, herbs, and spinach (cautiously—they both love nitrogen).

Foes: Beans, peas (nitrogen competition)

Cherry Tomatoes

Difficulty Level: Moderate

Best For: Containers, Small Spaces, Beginning Gardeners

Favorite Varieties:

- **Bumble Bee Mix:** A colorful, high-yield mix perfect for adding variety and vibrant color to your garden.
- **Chocolate Sprinkles:** These cherry-sized tomatoes bring a rich, complex flavor with a sweet kick.
- **Chocolate Cherry:** A rich, super cute shape! These beauties have an amazing flavor, with deep, chocolaty color and a sweet, complex taste that will make your garden pop.
- **Cherry Ember:** A favorite for flavor, these tomatoes are packed with sweetness and a hint of smokiness.

Growing Guide

- **Birthday:** about 7 days from seed
- **Days to Maturity:** 60-75 days
- **When to Start:** Transplant outdoors around May 15th
- **Special Spacing Requirements:** Space 12-18 inches apart
- **Light Requirements:** Full sun (8-12 hours minimum)

Special Care Notes

- Cherry tomatoes are a little easier to manage than larger varieties, but they still need consistent watering and good airflow.
- Prune lightly to avoid overcrowding, as cherry tomatoes can become bushy.

Harvesting

- **When to Harvest:** Ready when the tomatoes are fully colored and slightly soft to the touch.
- **How to Harvest:** Gently twist the fruit off or cut it with scissors to avoid damaging the plant.
- Storage tips: Best stored at room temperature to maintain flavor.

Pro Tips & Quirks

- Cherry tomatoes are often the first to ripen in the garden, which is why they're a great choice for beginners or those looking for early season rewards.

- They're perfect for snacking, salads, or garnishing dishes.
- For a continuous harvest, stagger planting dates or choose a variety with different maturity times.
- Cherry tomatoes are typically indeterminate, meaning they keep growing and producing fruit until the first frost. Keep up with pruning to prevent excessive vine growth and to ensure maximum yields.

Trellising & Pruning

Tomatoes are admittedly the garden star. There are dwarf varieties that need only staking and tying to support. But most vining tomatoes need solid support. Of your 15 minutes in the garden, these guys will take up most of your time but they are so gorgeous and generous—you will not mind. What makes these guys high maintenance? Pruning and trellising. If you are feeling adventurous and have extra time you can build a beautiful cattle panel trellis (plans below). This is effective but not a 15-minute task.

For a 15-minute friendly support, opt for as tall of a square tomato cage as you can find and press that into the soil the day you plant your plant. You can do serious damage to a plant trying to put the support in too late.

HOW TO BUILD A CATTLE PANNEL TRELLIS

Materials:
- 1 cattle panel (16 feet long, 50-52 inches tall)
- 2 T-posts (6-8 feet tall)
- Wire or zip ties
- Hammer or post-driver
- Gardening gloves

Steps:
1. **Set Up T-Posts:**
   o Place 1 T-post at each end of the 4-foot side of the 4x8 bed.
   o Drive them 2 feet into the ground, leaving 6-8 feet above ground.

2. **Position Cattle Panel:**
   o Bend the cattle panel into an arch and rest the ends on the T-posts.
   o Align the bottom of the panel with the edge of the bed.

3. **Secure the Panel:**

    o   Use wire or zip ties to attach the panel to the T-posts and make sure that it is stable.

4. **Plant Tomatoes:**

    o   Plant tomatoes at the base of the arch. As they grow, train them to climb the panel.

Pro Tip: Secure any loose spots with extra ties, and ensure the arch stays sturdy as your plants grow. You can do this for peas, cucumbers, beans, squash—any vining plant.

PRUNING TOMATOES IN 15 MINUTES

1. **Start Early:**

    ☐ Begin pruning once your tomato plants are about 1-2 feet tall. The earlier you start, the easier it is to manage.

2. **Remove Bottom Leaves:**

    ☐ Clip off any leaves that are touching the soil. These are prone to disease and can create a humid environment around the plant. Keep the lower 6-12 inches of the stem clean.

3. **Pinch Off Suckers:**

    ☐ Suckers are the small shoots that appear between the main stem and branches. Pinch these off early while they're small to prevent them from stealing energy from the main plant. (You'll notice them—they grow fast and furious!)

4. **Prunc for Airflow:**

    ☐ Remove any excess foliage in the middle of the plant to improve airflow. A healthier, airier plant is less likely to get fungal diseases.

5. **Focus on the Main Stem:**

    ☐ For indeterminate tomatoes, keep focusing on the main stem. Trim off any branches that grow below the first flower cluster. This helps direct energy to the fruit above.

6. **Clean Your Tools:**

   ☐ After each pruning session, wipe your scissors or pruners with rubbing alcohol to prevent the spread of disease.

7. **Aim for Consistency:**

   ☐ Aim to prune a little each week—don't wait until the vines are a tangled mess! A quick 15-minute session each time keeps things under control.

Pro Tip: Determinate tomatoes (also known as bush varieties) generally don't need much pruning. Here's why:

- **Determinate tomatoes** produce fruit on the main stem and branches, and they stop growing once they reach a certain height.
- **Pruning them too much** can reduce the number of flowers and fruit they produce since they don't have as much "vertical" growth as indeterminate types.

However, you can still remove:

- **Dead or diseased leaves** to keep the plant healthy.
- **Suckers** are growing at the base of the plant if they seem out of control and crawling on the ground. Other than that-don't cut too much!

Eggplant

Difficulty Level: Moderate

Best For: Medium to Large Spaces, Intermediate Gardeners

Favorite Varieties

- **Black Beauty:** Classic and reliable, this variety produces large, dark purple fruits with a mild, creamy texture-perfect for grilling or frying.
- **Fairy Tale:** These small, cute, striped eggplants have a sweet flavor and tender texture, making them perfect for grilling or roasting.
- **White Beauty:** An attractive white variety with a mild flavor, this eggplant is great for stuffing or as a fresh addition to Mediterranean dishes.

Growing Guide

- **Birthday:** 14 days from the day sown
- **Days to Maturity:** 60-80 days
- **When to Start:** Start indoors 8-10 weeks before the last frost and transplant once temperatures stay consistently above 70°F.
- **Special Spacing Requirements:** Space plants 18-24 inches apart
- **Light Requirements:** Full sun (6-8 hours minimum)

Special Care Notes

- Eggplants love heat, so make sure they get plenty of sunshine and are kept warm, especially during their early stages.
- Watering: Keep soil consistently moist, but avoid overwatering as eggplants are sensitive to soggy roots. A deep watering once or twice a week is usually best.
- Fertilizing: Use a balanced fertilizer during the growing season. Avoid high-nitrogen fertilizers, as they can result in lush foliage but poor fruit production.

Harvesting

- **When to Harvest:** Eggplant is ready when it has a glossy skin and is firm to the touch. It should be slightly soft but not mushy.
- **How to Harvest:** Cut the fruit from the plant with a sharp knife or pruners, leaving a small portion of the stem attached.
- **Storage tips:** Store harvested eggplants in a cool, dry place for up to a week but enjoy soon after harvest for the best flavor.

Pro Tips & Quirks

- Eggplant can be a bit fussy with temperature. If temperatures drop below 50°F at night, growth may slow down, and fruit production may decrease.
- Bitterness: Older or larger eggplants may have a more bitter taste. To reduce bitterness, cut the eggplant into slices, sprinkle with salt, and let it sit for about 30 minutes to draw out excess moisture. Rinse and pat dry before cooking.
- Pollination: Eggplant flowers are self-pollinating, but they'll do better with some gentle shaking of the plant to help the process.
- Eggplant plants are indeterminate, so they'll keep producing throughout the growing season until

the first frost hits. Keep up with regular harvesting to prevent overripe fruit from taking over the plant.

- Do you hate seedy eggplants? I don't sweat it, but I did know a woman who spent 15 min looking for eggplants with a dot on its blossom end—she swore they had fewer seeds. Some folks believe that a small dot at the blossom end (the bottom where the flower was) indicates a less mature, younger eggplant with fewer seeds. The reasoning is that a mature eggplant tends to develop a larger or more pronounced "scar" at the blossom end as it ages, while a younger one stays smooth with just a small dot. The theory is that the fewer the seeds, the more tender and less bitter the eggplant.

Friends: Like all members of this family, eggplant loves marigolds. The flower's strong sent repels pests. Herbs like basil and fragrant carrots all work together to provide the best eggplant.

Foes: Eggplant does not get along well with heavy feeders. Also this is one that will do best if you wait a week or two after the last frost to plant.

Potatoes

Difficulty Level: Moderate

Best For: Raised Beds, Containers, Root Cellaring

Favorite Varieties
- **Norland:** Early producer with red skin, great yield, and a solid performer.
- **Yukon Gold:** Creamy, buttery perfection-because who doesn't love a potato that basically comes pre-buttered?
- **Kennebec:** If you want a lot of potatoes with minimal fuss, this is your guy. Stores beautifully, too.

Growing Guide
- **Birthday:** 10-14 days from planting (a little patience goes a long way).
- **Days to Maturity:** 70-120 days, depending on variety and how well you keep up with hilling.
- **When to Start:** Plant 2-4 weeks before your last frost date, when the soil is at least 45°F. You read that right. You could have a freeze after putting these guys in the ground. I have had a potato crop

look completely obliterated but go on to produce HUNDREDS of pounds of potatoes. They are tougher than you might guess.

- **Special Spacing Requirements:** 12 inches apart, rows 2-3 feet apart.
- **Light Requirements:** Full sun (6-8 hours minimum).

Special Care Notes:

Alright, let's get real—potatoes are not a "plant it and forget it" crop. Traditionally sown, they are NOT 15-minute friendly. They need hilling, which is just a fancy way of saying, "Keep burying them over and over so they don't fail miserably." Potatoes form along the buried stem ABOVE the seed sown. So if you skip this step, your "harvest" will be sad and small. Also if the potato is exposed to light it will turn green and produce the toxin solanine. Sound familiar? It's a family trait to carry the potential toxin. That's why some people can't tolerate peppers and tomatoes. Back to potatoes. There are several methods that keep potatoes covered and are 15 minute friendly:

POPULAR HILLING METHODS

1. **Traditional Soil Hilling:** As the plant grows, mound up soil around the base, leaving just the top leaves showing. Repeat every couple of weeks.
2. **Straw Hilling:** Pile straw up to the crown of the plant. It creates an amazing loose environment for the potatoes and makes harvest ridiculously easy. Warning this method tends to attract slugs. Watch for that and put slug traps out if they are an issue.
3. **Compost Hilling:** Instead of plain soil, use compost for an extra nutrient boost while hilling. Double duty-feeding your plants while helping them grow more tubers.
4. **Grow Bags:** Perfect for small spaces and tight schedules! As the plant grows, just add more soil to the bag. Come harvest time, no digging required-just dump the bag out and collect your prize. Great for patios and raised beds where space and time is limited.

The Secret to the Best Harvest:
Let them DIE BACK COMPLETELY.

I know, it's tempting to yank them up early, but if you wait until the green leaves turn yellow, wilt, and look like an absolute disaster zone, that's when the real growth happens underground. After they die back, leave them in the soil for another two weeks to let the skins toughen up for storage.

Pests & Challenges:

Public Enemy #1: The Colorado Potato Beetle. This striped menace will chew your plants to nothing if given the chance. If you see them, it's time for battle. Frequent walks in the garden are your best friend when it comes to fighting this. It does not take long but it does take consistency.

Best Non-Toxic Pest Control:

- **Hand-picking & smashing:** Yep. It's exactly what it sounds like.
- **Soapy water spray:** A gentler way to deter them, though not always 100% effective.
- **Diatomaceous earth (DE):** Works, but I hesitate to use it because it kills ALL insects, even the ones we want around.
- **Trap Planting:** If I'm losing the war, I'll let one potato plant become a sacrificial lamb—the beetles will flock to it and just before they lay eggs, I pull the whole thing out and get rid of it. DO NOT let them get wings. Once they can fly, your whole garden is in trouble.
- **Foes: "It's not you—it is me."** Potatoes don't get along well with anyone. Keep these guys to themsleves. They attract pests, need special care, and take a lot of nutrients.
- **Friend: Calendula** can live well in the potato's shadow. Give enough space for hilling.

Wild to Wonderful: The Solanaceae Family's Sweet Gem

Physalis pruinosa (Aunt Molly's Ground Cherry)

Aunt Molly's Ground Cherry is a sweet, golden fruit with a delightful tropical flavor. Encased in a papery husk similar to a tomatillo, it's a forager's treasure. However, caution is advised: like other members of the Solanaceae family, it contains **solanine,** a substance that can be toxic in large quantities. To enjoy this fruit safely, make sure it is fully ripe—typically when it naturally falls to the ground.

Celery

Parsnips

Apiaceae

Carrot Family

These plants love cool seasons, consistent water, and, most importantly, they are super easy keepers. Water them well, and they'll reward you with a great harvest.

Dill

Cilantro

Carrot

Fennel

Bulb

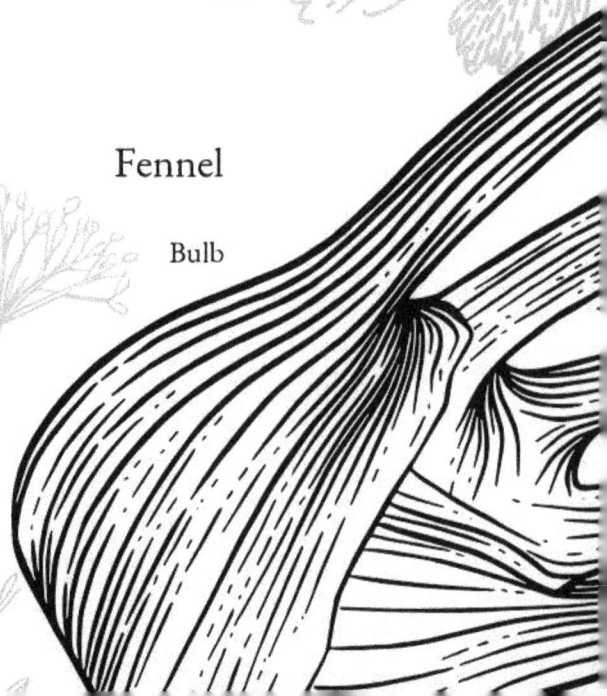

APIACEAE

Rooted Treasure—Carrot Family

Difficulty Level: Easy to Moderate. Best For: Cool-season gardens, succession planting

Common Family Traits:

These easy-keeping plants share traits of Feathery foliage: tap roots or hollow stems, umbrella-shaped flower clusters, and aromatic qualities.

Growing Conditions Specific to This Family

- Temperature: 55°F-75°F (13°C-24°C)
- Light: Full sun, tolerates partial shade in warm climates
- Soil: Loose, sandy, well-drained soil
- Space: These plants often make great "middle plants" in your garden. Not too tall and not too short, they fit nicely into spaces that need filling but aren't overpowered by taller or more aggressive growers.

Friends: Apiaceae plants work well with plants like **onions** and **tomatoes**. They can help repel certain pests like aphids and carrot flies.

Foes: Avoid planting them near **dill**, which can inhibit their growth. Keep them in separate raised beds.

Special Considerations

Requires consistently loose soil to develop good roots—broad fork will aerate bed without disturbing soil layers. Celery and carrots are also prone to **root rot** in overly wet or compacted soil. Make sure your beds drain well and monitor for pests regularly. Watch out for pests like **carrot flies**, aphids, and slugs, which can damage the roots or leaves.

Family members include: carrots, celery, parsley, parsnips.

Fun Fact: Celery root (celeriac) is an often-overlooked family member that adds wonderful earthy flavors to soups and stews.

Carrots

Difficulty Level: Moderate

Best For: Succession planting, winter storage

Favorite Varieties

- Napoli F1 (High Mountain Mowing): Fast-growing, great for overwintering
- Tendersweet (True Leaf Market): Sweeter taste, longer growing period

Growing Guide

- **Birthday:** about 20 days from planting.
- **Days to Maturity:** 56-75+ days
- **When to Start:** Direct sow after last frost for summer harvest, mid-summer for fall/winter crop
- **Special Spacing:** Carrots are small, so they need to be spaced 30 seeds per foot. You can use a seeding tool—or a careful hand—to ensure the spacing is even, which will make thinning easier.
- Depth: Surface to 1/4 inch deep

Special Care Notes

- Carrots are not quite garden divas but a little TLC goes a long way for a good harvest.
- **Watering**: Keep your carrot bed consistently moist, especially during germination. Cover your seeds with a **board** or **cloth** to maintain moisture, but **remove the cover once the seeds sprout** (typically in about **3 weeks**). This "covering" technique is a great way to prevent the soil from drying out, which is crucial when growing carrots, as their tiny seeds are planted near the surface. However, remove the cover **once sprouted**, as leaving it on too long can damage fragile seedlings.
- **Thinning**: While thinning is essential for healthy carrot growth, it can be tricky because the seedlings are delicate. So, I recommend **sowing sparingly** to minimize the need for thinning.
- **Weeding**: Carrots are susceptible to weeds because of their long germination period. So it's important to keep your beds weed-free. Using a board to cover the seeds helps block weed growth near the carrots, but make sure to cultivate thoroughly around the board to prevent weeds from taking over your bed.

Harvesting

- **Ready to harvest:** When roots reach desired size (usually 1/2-3/4 inch diameter at crown). Timing depends on variety and is varied. Typically **Napoli:** 56+ days after sprouting. **Tendersweet:** 75+ days after sprouting.
- **Method:** Loosen the soil with broadfork or shovel before pulling. Avoid pulling tops when harvesting. Push carrot down to break roots and then pull up.
- **Storage:** Can remain in the ground under straw in zones 6 and below. Also cn be stored in the root cellar.
- **Winter Bonus:** Flavor improves after frost

Pro Tips & Quirks

- Mix your carrot seeds with equal parts of sand before sowing. This helps ensure even distribution and prevents planting too many seeds in one spot. A special recipe for cornstarch slurry—for perfect carrot sowing—is included at the end of this section.
- Despite popular advice, avoid companion planting with radishes—This just makes for a messy, complicated, and usually unsuccessful harvest.
- Thin carefully to prevent disturbing the remaining plants.
- Can be overwintered under straw for spring harvest.

Friends: Carrots are pretty likeable. They pair well with lettuce, onions, beans, and tomatoes.
Foes: Don't crowd. Don't plant with deep rooted veggies. Carrots send out taproots to tell how much room they have to grow.

Common Mistakes to Avoid

- **Transplanting**—This doesn't work well without expensive systems (#askmehowIknow). If you want crazy carrots, densely scatter seeds and then try to thin them out by shoveling them to another bed. Funkiest pretzel knot carrots I ever grew (don't do it).
- **Overcrowding**—this produces skinny, stunted carrots that even "baby carrots" would reject.
- **Heavy/compacted soil**—Carrots have long taproots, so it's important to **loosen the soil** well before planting. If your soil is compacted, add **sand** or **compost** to improve tilth.
- **Poor germination**—Letting the seed dry out is the #1 cause. These tiny seeds sit on the surface of the soil. If they sprout and then the soil dries the seed will never grow. So keep the soil moist, especially in the early stages. Do not spray the bed directly though or you'll move that tiny seed and it will not thrive in the cracks of your raised bed.

Harvest and Storage

Carrots saved for storage in bed can rot and attract mice. Check your crop regularly. The easiest will covering your raised bed and harvesting as you need but to be safe I would plan to have your bed fully harvested by the end of the year.

Celery

Difficulty Level: Moderate to Advanced Best For: Cool season gardens, patient gardeners

Favorite Varieties

- **Tall Utah:** Strong stalks, great flavor
- **Tendercrisp:** Self-blanching variety with crisp, tender stalks
- **Local varieties:** Starting from transplant is best. If your local garden store doesn't have my favorite variety, don't sweat it. You'll have a significant advantage by planting healthy starts.

Growing Guide

- **Birthday:** about 20-30 days from seed.
- **Days to Maturity:** 85-120 days, depending on the variety.
- **When to Start:** Spring or fall for cool-weather growing. Celery thrives in temperatures between 55-75°F (13-24°C).
- **Spacing:** Ideally, space plants 8-12 inches apart in rows about 18 inches apart. Celery needs room for its stalks to grow tall and straight.
- **Special Planting Tip:** Plant the oval base sideways or at a slight angle to fit plants closer together (about 8 inches apart) in smaller spaces.

Special Care Notes

- Must maintain consistent moisture (shallow roots)
- Heavy feeder requiring additional nitrogen
- Needs side-dressing every 3-4 weeks after 6" height
- pH requirement: 6.0-7.0
- Benefits from blanching (covering stalks)

Harvesting

- **Ready to Harvest:** When stalks are 8-12 inches tall—and crunchy.
- **How to Harvest:**
  - Cut the entire plant at the base.
  - Or, snip the outer stalks individually to allow the inner ones to grow.
- **Timing of Harvest** for the best flavor: Before the plant flowers (bolts) or extreme heat arrives.
- **Storage:** Wrap in damp paper towels and store in the refrigerator for up to 2 weeks. For longer storage, celery can be blanched and frozen.
- **Tall Utah:** Best harvested when stalks reach 10-12 inches tall for optimal crunch and flavor.
- **Tendercrisp:** Ideal when stalks are 8-10 inches tall; self-blanching ensures tender texture without additional effort.

Pro Tips & Quirks

- Bitter celery is still useful for soups/dehydrating
- **Time Saver:** Celery can be finicky to start from seed. For beginners, I highly recommend purchasing **celery starts** from a local nursery or garden center for a smoother and more reliable start.
- **Self-Blanching:** Another reason celery can become bitter is not blanching during the growing period (the base is covered and only the leafy greens are exposed). I love **self-blanching varieties** because they save you the extra step.
- To avoid diseases like blight and fungal infections, use **drip irrigation** or a **soaker hose** to water at the base of the plant, keeping the leaves dry. Mulching the soil can help maintain moisture and keep the soil cooler, which celery loves.

Friends: Celery pairs well with slow-growing neighbors like marigolds, potatoes, or tomatoes. These plants grow big after celery has had a chance to establish, providing benefits like weed suppression and moisture retention.

Foes: These guys have a bit of a family feud brewing. Avoid planting it with carrots or parsley as they compete for similar nutrients.

Cilantro

Difficulty Level: Easy to Moderate

Best For: Cool-season gardens, container gardening, beginners

Cilantro is a heat-sensitive herb that rewards quick action and regular harvests. Focus on planting in spring and fall, selecting slow-bolt varieties for the longest-lasting yields. Whether you're using it fresh or growing it for seeds, cilantro's versatility makes it a valuable addition to any garden. Beginners can enjoy success by sowing seeds directly and keeping the plants cool and moist. Happy gardening!

Favorite Varieties

- **Calypso:** A slow-bolting variety with strong, fresh flavor and long-lasting leaves.
- **Slow Bolt Cilantro** (from True Leaf Market): Specifically bred to resist bolting in hot weather, providing extended leaf harvest.
- **Local Varieties:** Great for adapting to regional conditions; check your garden store for recommendations.

Growing Guide

- **Birthday:** about 5-10 days from seed.
- **Days to Maturity:** 50-70 days.
- **When to Start:** Early spring or late summer for cool-weather growth. Cilantro struggles in extreme heat.
- **Spacing:** Plant 6-8 inches apart in rows spaced 12-18 inches apart. Good air circulation helps prevent disease.
- **Light Requirements:** Full sun in cooler weather; partial shade in hotter climates to extend the growing season.

Special Care Notes

- **Watering:** Keep the soil consistently moist but not soggy. Avoid overwatering, as cilantro dislikes sitting in wet soil.
- **Soil Requirements:** Cilantro thrives in well-drained soil rich in organic matter with a pH between 6.2-6.8.
- **Temperature Sensitivity:** This herb bolts quickly in hot weather. Plant in spring and fall to avoid

mid-summer heat, or provide shade during hotter months.

- **Fertilization:** Not a heavy feeder but benefits from a light application of compost or organic fertilizer at planting time.

Harvesting

- **Ready to Harvest:** When leaves are 3-4 inches tall.
- **How to Harvest:**
  - Snip the outer leaves first to encourage new growth.
  - Harvest frequently to maintain tender leaves and delay bolting.
- **Timing of Harvest:** Pick leaves before the plant starts to flower (bolts). Once bolted, leaves may taste bitter.
- **Storage Tips:** Use fresh for the best flavor. Alternatively, chop and freeze in ice cube trays with water for later use.

Pro Tips & Quirks

- **Bolting:** Opt for slow-bolt varieties to prolong harvests in warmer weather.
- **Seedling Tips:** Cilantro does not transplant well. Sow seeds directly into the garden or container for best results.
- **Double Duty:** Once cilantro bolts, let the flowers attract pollinators, and harvest the seeds (coriander) for cooking or replanting.
- **Companion Planting:** Grow near tomatoes or summer squash to provide shade during hotter months.

Friends: Basil, parsley, tomatoes, and summer squash. These companions enhance growth and repel pests.

Foes: Fennel, as it can inhibit cilantro growth.

Culantro—rumored to be the "non-soap-tasting" version of cilantro—has been popping up in garden centers lately. It's gaining attention for its ability to give you that familiar cilantro flavor without the soapy aftertaste. If you like cilantro, you might not notice much of a difference, but culantro could be a great option to try if you're looking for a less "soap" flavored herb in your garden. Worth a shot if you're into experimenting with your herb garden! A perennial in zone 10, this herb will not thrive in cooler climates.

Dill

Difficulty Level: Easy

Best For: Companion planting, herb gardens, pickling

Dill is an easy-to-grow herb that offers versatility in the kitchen and value in the garden. Its feathery leaves, fragrant flowers, and flavorful seeds make it a favorite for pickling and seasoning. Beginners will appreciate its low-maintenance nature and ability to self-seed. Whether growing dill for culinary uses or as a companion plant, its presence will enhance any garden space.

Favorite Varieties

- **Bouquet:** Tall stems, feathery leaves, good for fresh and dry use.
- **Fernleaf:** Compact and slower to bolt, making it ideal for containers. Lots of flavorful fronds.
- **Dukat:** A hardy variety with excellent flavor, and prolific seed heads for preserving.

Growing Guide

- **Birthday:** about 7-14 days from seed.
- **Days to Maturity:** 40-70 days, depending on the variety.
- **When to Start:** Direct sow seeds outdoors after the last frost date.
- **Spacing:** Space plants 12-18 inches apart in rows, allowing for good airflow and growth.
- **Light Requirements:** Full sun for optimal growth.

Special Care Notes

- **Vertical Support:** Dill is a tall plant, so it doesn't require as much horizontal space, but it definitely takes up vertical space, so consider planting it along a trellis or near taller plants, like tomatoes or cucumbers.
- **Fertilization:** Minimal fertilization is needed as excessive nutrients can reduce the flavor intensity. This is why you can plant with nutrient hogs like cucumbers and it still thrives.

Harvesting

- **When to Harvest:** Begin harvesting leaves when plants reach about 12 inches tall.
- **How to Harvest:**
    - Snip fresh fronds (leaves) as needed for cooking.

- Collect flowers and seeds once the plant matures for pickling or drying. The flowers become an abundant source of seed heads. This is a crop in and of itself. Save for the spice, dill seed, next year's garden planting, and pickles.
- **Timing of Harvest:** Regularly harvest to encourage continuous growth.
- **Storage Tips:** Best used fresh but can be dried or frozen for later use. To dry the dill, hang it upside down in a cool, dry place.

Pro Tips & Quirks
- **Direct Sow Only:** Dill has a delicate root system and doesn't transplant well. Start seeds directly in the garden or container.
- **Tall Growth:** Plan your garden layout with its height in mind to avoid shading smaller plants.
- **Morning Watering:** Water in the morning to reduce the risk of fungal issues.

Friends: Cucumbers, carrots, zucchini, beans (dill attracts beneficial insects and repels pests). Dill is super tall so when considering it's friends remember that it will cast a shadow depending on the direction of your garden. It's frilly enough for that to be insignificant if the plants around it are fully leafed. The time to consider this is when you are trying to sow a second crop

Foes: Avoid planting near fennel, as the two herbs can cross-pollinate and compete for nutrients.

Fennel

Difficulty Level: Easy (from transplant), Moderate (from seed)
Best For: Herb gardens, culinary enthusiasts, pollinator-friendly gardens

Fennel is a versatile and rewarding plant that fits well in both herb and vegetable gardens. Whether you're growing it for the flavorful bulbs or the delicate fronds, this plant adds a unique touch to your cooking and attracts beneficial pollinators to your garden. Beginners can focus on frond varieties for easier growing, while seasoned gardeners will enjoy the challenge of cultivating perfect bulbs. Happy planting!

Favorite Varieties

- **Finocchio:** A classic bulbing variety with a sweet, anise-like flavor. Perfect for dishes like pasta, marinara, or Thanksgiving recipes.
- **Fernleaf:** Compact, grown for its feathery fronds rather than bulbs. Ideal for garnishes, salads, and gardeners with limited space.
- **Sweet Florence:** Known for its delicate greens and mild flavor, this variety is excellent for frond-focused gardeners.

Growing Guide

- **Birthday:** about 8-12 days from seed.
- **Days to Maturity:** 90-115 days.
- **When to Start:** Direct sow in early spring, about 4-6 weeks before the last frost, or in late summer for a fall harvest.
- **Spacing:** 10 inches apart for bulbs, but you can plant closer (6 inches) if harvesting early for smaller bulbs or greens.
- **Light Requirements:** Full sun is best, but fennel can tolerate partial shade in hotter climates.

Special Care Notes

- **Watering:** Keep soil consistently moist but not soggy. Deep watering is key to developing large, firm bulbs. Avoid wetting foliage to reduce the risk of fungal issues.
- **Soil Requirements:** Prefers well-drained soil rich in organic matter, with a pH between 6.0–7.0. Amend soil with compost before planting.
- **Fertilization:** Light feeding works best. A side dressing of organic compost or a mild nitrogen boost helps bulbs swell. Avoid over-fertilizing, as it can reduce flavor.
- **Temperature Sensitivity:** Fennel thrives in cooler weather but can tolerate summer heat if watered consistently.

Harvesting

- **When to Harvest:** Bulbs are ready when they reach 3-4 inches in diameter and feel firm. Fronds can be snipped throughout the growing season.
- **How to Harvest:**
  - For bulbs: Cut at the base with a sharp knife.
  - For fronds: Use scissors to snip leaves as needed without harming the plant.

- **Storage Tips:** Wrap fronds in a damp towel or store in a plastic bag in the fridge for up to a week. Bulbs can be kept in a cool, dark place for several weeks.

Pro Tips & Quirks

- **Direct Sow vs. Transplant:** This is a controversial opinion, but I always start from transplants so I can get a more mature plant in the garden sooner in the spring.
- **Dual Purpose:** Enjoy fennel for both its bulbs and its fronds. Use fronds as garnishes or seasoning while waiting for bulbs to develop.
- **Re-sprouting:** Bulbs may regrow if roots are left in the ground, but they'll produce frond-like greens rather than another bulb.

Friends: Dill, cucumbers, lettuce, and tomatoes. Fennel attracts pollinators and beneficial insects.

Foes: Avoid planting near carrots or cilantro as it can inhibit their growth.

Parsnip

Difficulty Level: Moderate

Best For: Cool-weather gardens, root vegetable enthusiasts, roasting recipes

Parsnips are a rewarding root vegetable that shine in cool-weather gardens. Their sweet, nutty flavor makes them a favorite for roasting and for soups—especially after a frost. With a bit of patience and proper care, you'll enjoy a delicious harvest that is worth the wait, perfect for both fall and overwintering crops. If you plant again Late summer (August or around 10–12 weeks before your first frost), you can expect the growing to "pause" and then grow again as temperatures warm in March and April.

Favorite Varieties

- **All American Parsnip:** A classic variety known for its long, sweet roots, ideal for roasting and cooler climates.
- **Hollow Crown:** An heirloom variety with excellent flavor and uniform roots, perfect for soups and stews.
- **Gladiator:** A hybrid known for its disease resistance and smooth, tender roots.

Growing Guide

- **Birthday:** about 15-20 days from seed.

- **Days to Maturity:** 100-120 days.

- **When to Start:** Direct sow seeds in early spring, 4-6 weeks before the last frost, or in late summer for an overwinter crop.

- **Spacing:** Sow seeds 1-2 inches apart, then thin seedlings to 3-4 inches apart once they're a few inches tall.

- **Light Requirements:** Full sun to partial shade.

- **Slow going:** Like carrots, parsnips can take anywhere from 2 to 4 week to sprout, depending on the temperature. Once they sprout, they'll be small but mighty! Also, like their orange cousin, the sprout is thin, green, and delicate—like fine blades of grass.

Special Care Notes

- **Watering:** Keep soil evenly moist but not waterlogged. Parsnips require consistent moisture to develop straight, healthy roots.

- **Soil Requirements:** Loose, well-drained soil free of rocks and debris to prevent misshapen roots. A pH of 6.0-6.8 is ideal.

- **Temperature Sensitivity:** Parsnips thrive in cool weather and can tolerate light frosts, which enhance their sweetness.

Harvesting

- **When to Harvest:** Roots are ready when they reach 1-2 inches in diameter, typically in late fall or early winter.

- **How to Harvest:** Use a garden fork to gently loosen the soil around the roots before pulling them up. Take care not to damage the roots.

- **Timing of Harvest:** For the sweetest flavor, wait until after the first frost to harvest. Frost converts starches into sugars, enhancing their taste.

- **Storage Tips:** Store parsnips in a cool, moist environment such as a root cellar or refrigerator. They can also be left in the ground and harvested as needed during winter, provided the soil doesn't freeze solid.

Pro Tips & Quirks

- **Patience is Key:** Parsnips are slow to germinate (2-4 weeks). Be patient and keep the soil moist during this time.

- **Overwintering:** Plant late-summer crops for overwintering. Growth will pause in cold months and resume in spring, providing an early harvest.

- **Rodent Alert:** Watch for rodent activity, as parsnips are a favorite snack for mice and moles.

- **Sprout Appearance:** Parsnip seedlings resemble fine blades of grass—don't mistake them for weeds!

Friends: Onions, garlic, and radishes. These companions can deter pests and promote healthy growth.

Foes: Avoid planting near carrots, as they can attract similar pests like carrot flies.

Sunflower

Easy
Grower

Marigolds

Asteraceae

Lettuce Family

Butter
Lettuce

Romaine

Endive

Zinnia

ASTERACEAE

Leaves of Plenty

- **Lettuce** *(Butter, Romaine, Mesclun Mix, Radicchio, Endive)*
- **Calendula** *(Edible flowers and pollinatorfriendly plant)*
- **Marigolds** *(Pest deterrent and pollinator magnet)*
- **Zinnias** *(Bold colors and easy-to-grow cut flowers)*
- **Sunflowers** *(Single-stem, branching, and edible seed varieties)*
- **Gazania** *(Hardy, sun-loving blooms for borders and containers)*

General Characteristics

The Asteraceae family, also known as the Lettuce Family, is the beginner gardener's best friend. This low-fuss family includes plants that thrive in cool seasons and appreciate consistent watering. These plants are easy to grow and maintain, rewarding gardeners with abundant harvests when given proper care.

Growing Conditions Specific to This Family

Members of this family prefer loose, fertile, and well-drained soil. Adding organic compost or aged manure enhances soil structure and fertility. They grow best in temperatures ranging from 45°F (7°C) to 75°F (24°C), making them ideal for early spring and fall planting. Most require 8 hours of sunlight daily but can tolerate partial shade in hot climates. These light lovers usually have tiny seeds that should be planted near the surface—just press lightly into the soil.

Common Family Traits

- Cool-season lovers
- Compact, low-growing plants
- Thrive in well-drained, nutrient-rich soil
- Require consistent watering to keep the soil evenly moist

Friends & Foes (Family Level)

Friends: Plants like carrots, radishes, and cucumbers make excellent companions. These pairings provide shade, deter pests, and optimize garden space.

Foes: Avoid planting Asteraceae members near Brassicas (e.g., cabbage, broccoli) as they may compete for similar nutrients, potentially hindering each other's growth.

Special Considerations for This Family

Temperature and Light:

These plants struggle in hot weather. Lettuce, in particular, can become bitter when exposed to excessive heat. Ensure plenty of light for germination but provide light shade during the hottest parts of the day in summer. Plant behind sunflowers. Light is available when germination for lettuce is needed but the sunflower is tall and offers shade when the summer sun is hottest.

Beginner-Proof Pest Tips:

- **Pests:** Watch out for aphids, slugs, and snails, which can damage leaves and stunt growth.
- **Diseases:** Overly wet conditions can lead to downy mildew and leaf spot. Ensure proper airflow and avoid overhead watering to reduce risks.
- **Bonus Tip:** Plant marigolds nearby to repel aphids naturally.

Prevention Tips:

- **Harvest Young Leaves:** Pick leaves early to avoid rot that attracts pests.
- **Slug Traps:** Use traps filled with beer or water mixed with yeast to manage slugs without harming plants.
- **Spacing and Airflow:** Proper plant spacing improves air circulation and prevents moisture build-up, reducing disease risk.

Watering and Fertilization:

Aim for about an inch of water a week—this typically means a good soaking once a week. However, in warm weather, watering smaller amounts more frequently keeps lettuce sweeter. Lettuce and other Asteraceae plants are light feeders but benefit from nutrient-rich soil. Amend with organic compost at planting time for optimal growth.

The Asteraceae family offers incredible diversity. Experiment with colors and textures you haven't tried before! Pungent varieties like escarole and kale mellow beautifully when cooked in soups. Don't rule out a variety because of an experience—this family has some real winners worth revisiting. With their quick payoff and nutritional punch, Asteraceae plants are a beginner gardener's delight.

Lettuce

Difficulty Level: Easy

Best For: Beginner gardeners, salad lovers, compact spaces

This family is a versatile, easy-to-grow crop that thrives in cooler weather. With proper spacing, regular watering, and the right varieties, you can enjoy tender, flavorful leaves for salads, wraps, and more. Succession planting ensures a steady supply, while companion planting adds diversity and protection to your garden.

Favorite Varieties

- **Buttercrunch:** A tender, buttery-textured lettuce with a mild flavor, perfect for salads.
- **Mignonette:** Slow-bolting, heat-tolerant, and colorful. Can be harvested as baby lettuce or grown into larger heads. Cold hardy.
- **Heatwave Mix:** A blend of heat-resistant baby lettuce varieties that resist bitterness during warmer weather.

Growing Guide

- **Birthday:** about 3 days from seed.
- **Days to Maturity:** 45-60 days, depending on the variety. Sooner for baby greens.
- **When to Start:** Sow seeds in early spring or late summer for cool-season crops. For continuous harvest, sow every 2-3 weeks.
- **Spacing:** Space plants 8-12 inches apart in rows 12-18 inches apart to ensure proper air circulation and healthy growth.
- **Light Requirements:** Prefers partial shade in warm climates or full sun in cooler seasons.

Special Care Notes

- **Watering:** Maintain consistent moisture, but avoid overwatering to prevent rot. Morning watering is best.
- **Soil Requirements:** Loose, well-drained soil rich in organic matter. A pH of 6.0-7.0 is ideal.
- **Temperature Sensitivity:** Protect from extreme heat with shade cloth or by planting near taller crops.

Harvesting

- **When to Harvest:** Leaves are ready when they reach 4 inches in length. For head varieties, harvest when heads are firm and fully formed.
- **How to Harvest:** Snip outer leaves for a continuous harvest or cut the entire plant at the base for head varieties.
- **Timing of Harvest:** In the morning for the crispest, most flavorful leaves.
- **Storage Tips:** Store harvested lettuce in the refrigerator, wrapped in a damp paper towel or in a breathable bag, for up to a week.

Pro Tips & Quirks

- **Pest Management:** Watch for slugs and aphids. Use organic solutions like row covers, beer traps, diatomaceous earth (use cautiously) or companion plants like marigolds to deter pests.

BITTER LETTUCE: KEEPING IT SWEET IN THE HEAT

What is Bolting?

Bolting refers to when a plant prematurely sends up a flower stalk and goes to seed, often resulting in a tough, bitter-tasting crop. This typically happens in cool-season vegetables like lettuce, spinach, and cilantro when they are exposed to heat or long daylight hours, signaling them to complete their lifecycle. Instead of growing nice, tender leaves, they focus all their energy on flowering and seed production.

Why Does It Happen?

Bolting is a natural survival mechanism for plants. When they experience stress from high temperatures or excessive sunlight, they quickly shift to reproduction mode, trying to produce seeds before they die.
This is most common in spring or early summer when plants that prefer cooler weather suddenly face rising temperatures.

Bolting Prevention:

1. **Choose Heat-Resistant Varieties**: Some plants are bred specifically to resist bolting in warmer conditions. Varieties like 'Boltardy' beets, 'Tyee' spinach, and 'Butterhead' lettuce are designed to thrive longer in heat. When choosing seeds, look for descriptions mentioning heat tolerance or slow bolting.

2. **Provide Shade**: Excessive sun is one of the primary triggers for bolting. During the hottest part of the day, you can shade plants by using floating row covers, shade cloth, or even strategically placing taller crops nearby to provide some relief. A little afternoon shade can go a long way to delay bolting.

3. **Keep Soil Moist**: Stress from drought or inconsistent watering can encourage bolting. Keeping the soil evenly moist (but not waterlogged) can help regulate the plant's stress levels. Irrigation (a watering system like drip hoses set to a timer) is your 15-minute gardener friend. While I find nothing as relaxing as watering, it is also stressful when the garden depends solely on you for it.

4. **Succession Planting**: Since bolting is inevitable once temperatures rise, stagger your plantings in smaller batches every couple of weeks to ensure a continuous harvest of tender, flavorful crops before they bolt.

5. **Timing is Key**: Plant cool-season crops early in the spring, giving them enough time to mature before the heat sets in. If you're growing in hotter climates, consider planting in the fall when temperatures are milder.

6. **Pinch Off Flower Buds Early**: If you catch the plant starting to bolt, pinch off any flower buds as soon as you see them. While this won't stop the process entirely, it may slow it down and allow the plant to keep producing leaves for a little longer.

Radicchio

Difficulty Level: Moderate

Best For: Season extension, colorful salads, cooler climates

Radicchio is a vibrant, versatile addition to any garden, bringing both color and unique flavor to your table. Its tolerance for frost makes it an excellent season extender, and its bitter-sweet taste adds a gourmet touch to salads and dishes. With the right care and timing, radicchio can be a rewarding crop for gardeners looking to diversify their harvest.

Favorite Variety

- **Palla Rossa:** A popular variety with deep red leaves and a slightly bitter, crunchy texture. Perfect for adding color and complexity to salads, especially when combined with milder greens like buttercrunch lettuce.

Growing Guide

- **Birthday:** about 5-10 days from seed.
- **Days to Maturity:** 70-90 days
- **When to Start:** Sow seeds 8-10 weeks before the last frost for a spring crop or in late summer for a fall harvest.
- **Spacing:** Sow 2-3 seeds every 8-12 inches, and thin to the strongest plant. Rows should be spaced 12-18 inches apart for ample air circulation and tight head formation.
- **Light Requirements:** Full sun to partial shade, especially in warmer climates.

Special Care Notes

- **Soil Requirements:** Prefers well-drained, nutrient-rich soil with a pH of 6.0-7.5. Add compost before planting for the best results.
- **Temperature Sensitivity:** Thrives in cooler weather and tolerates frost, which enhances its sweetness. Protect from excessive heat with a shade cloth.

Harvesting

- **When to Harvest:** Heads are ready when they are firm, compact, and deeply colored. Outer leaves should fully wrap the head.
- **How to Harvest:** Cut at the base with a sharp knife when the head feels firm to the touch.
- **Timing of Harvest:** In the morning for the crispest leaves. If grown for baby greens, pick individual leaves as needed.
- **Storage Tips:** Store whole heads in the refrigerator for up to two weeks. Wrap in a damp paper towel to retain freshness.

Pro Tips & Quirks

- **Frost Sweetens Flavor:** Exposure to frost breaks down starches into sugars, reducing bitterness and enhancing flavor.
- **Succession Planting:** Sow seeds every few weeks during the growing season to extend your harvest window.
- **Companion Planting:** Pairs well with carrots, onions, and garlic, which help deter pests. Avoid planting near other brassicas like cabbage, to reduce competition.
- **Pest Management:** Keep an eye out for slugs and aphids. Use organic solutions like neem oil or diatomaceous earth to control infestations.

Endive

Difficulty Level: Moderate

Best For: Mixed salads, cooler seasons, textured greens

Endive is a versatile, hardy addition to any cool-season garden. Its slightly tangy flavor and unique texture make it a favorite for mixed salads, while its frost tolerance ensures a longer growing season.

Favorite Variety

- **Frisee:** Known for its curly, frilly leaves, this variety adds texture and a slight tang to mixed salads. It pairs beautifully with sweeter greens like buttercrunch lettuce for a balanced flavor and a light crunch.

Growing Guide

- **Birthday:** about 7-14 days from seed.
- **Days to Maturity:** 50-75 days
- **When to Start:** Sow seeds in early spring or late summer for cooler season harvests.
- **Spacing:** Space plants 8-10 inches apart, with rows 12 inches apart to ensure proper air circulation and healthy growth.
- **Light Requirements:** Full sun to partial shade, especially in warmer climates.

Special Care Notes

- **Soil Requirements:** Prefers well-drained, nutrient-rich soil with a pH of 6.0-7.0. Add compost before planting to boost growth.
- **Temperature Sensitivity:** Thrives in cool weather and can tolerate light frost. Protect from extreme heat with shade cloth or strategic placement near taller plants.

Harvesting

- **When to Harvest:** Endive is ready to harvest when heads are full, and leaves are vibrant green or yellow, depending on the variety.
- **How to Harvest:** For head varieties, cut the entire plant at the base. For loose-leaf types, pick the outer leaves first to allow continued growth.
- **Timing of Harvest:** In the morning for the crispest leaves. Avoid harvesting during hot afternoons.

- **Storage Tips:** Store in the refrigerator for up to one week. Wrap in a damp paper towel to retain freshness.

Pro Tips & Quirks

- **Frost Enhances Flavor:** A light frost can improve the taste of the endive, making it an excellent crop for fall or winter gardens.
- **Succession Planting:** Sow seeds every few weeks to ensure a continuous harvest throughout the season.
- **Companion Planting:** Pairs well with radicchio, another cool-season green, and lettuce like Mignonette for a beautiful salad bowl.
- **Pest Management:** Watch for slugs and snails. Use natural deterrents like crushed eggshells or non-toxic dish soap spray.

Pro Tip:

Endive is wonderful in lettuce mixes. Frost enhances its flavor, making it a fantastic addition to your winter or fall garden. Pair it with **Mignonette,** that beautiful speckled lettuce, which thrives in cooler weather for gorgeous greens all season long.

The Flowery Side

I lean heavily into flowers found in the Asteraceae family. These happy little (and large) blooms get along with so many and add more than beauty. Sunflowers offer shade in the hottest summer months and provide some protection when planted near heat-sensitive veggies like lettuces or late-blooming brassicas. Remember, don't put tall sunflowers where sunloving neighbors (like tomatoes or peppers) will get grumpy in its shade.

Calendula

Difficulty Level: Easy

Best For: Beginner gardeners looking for vibrant, edible flowers that also have medicinal uses.

Favorite Varieties

- Resina: Known for its resinous petals, perfect for making soothing salves.
- Pacific Beauty: A mix of bright orange and yellow blooms that add a pop of color to any garden.

Growing Guide

- **Birthday:** about 7-10 days from seed.
- **Days to Maturity:** 50-60 days
- **When to Start:** Start indoors 6-8 weeks before the last frost, or sow directly outdoors after the frost danger has passed.
- **Special Spacing Requirements:** Space plants 10-12 inches apart to allow for airflow.
- **Light Requirements:** Full sun, but they can tolerate partial shade.

Special Care Notes

Calendulas thrive in well-drained, nutrient-rich soil with a slightly acidic pH. They prefer cooler temperatures and will struggle in hot, dry weather. Keep them watered regularly but avoid letting them sit in soggy soil. I love putting these guys on the edges of my garden where I can pick regularly and they don't mind getting a little shaded. These guys also love potatoes.

Harvesting

- **When to Harvest**: When the flowers are fully open, typically in late spring to early summer.
- **How to Harvest:** Snip off flowers with clean scissors, and always leave some blooms on the plant for continuous growth.
- **Storage Tips:** Dry flowers by hanging them upside down or using a dehydrator to preserve them for later use in teas or ointments. The skin salve is absolutely dreamy for boo-boos and your kids will absolutely DELIGHT in making a cream they "grew".

Pro Tips & Quirks

- Calendulas attract beneficial insects, like ladybugs, which help control pests in your garden.
- **Common mistake**: Overwatering. Calendulas don't like to have "wet feet," so ensure good drainage. We love edging our potato and tomato beds with these.

Friend: EVERYONE. Carrots, Potatoes, Tomatoes, Peppers, and Eggplant especially benefit from the way calendula repels flea beetles and aphids.

Foes: Beans can be stunted if planted close to Calendula. Note that calendula can act as a trap crop. This means that the bugs that love your veggies love calendula more and if you are growing for the blooms alone, consider making a separate herb patch. I have only experienced the repelling powers of calendula so I personally do not worry about it.

Marigolds

Difficulty Level: Easy

Best For: Gardeners looking for vibrant, pest-repelling flowers with minimal care.

Favorite Varieties:

- **African Marigold:** A large, bright orange flower perfect for adding bold color.
- **French Marigold:** Smaller and more compact, with a variety of colors, including red, yellow, and orange.

Growing Guide:

- **Birthday:** about 5-10 days from seed.
- **Days to Maturity:** 50-60 days
- **When to Start:** Start indoors 6-8 weeks before the last frost or sow directly outdoors after the danger of frost has passed.
- **Special Spacing Requirements:** Space plants 8-12 inches apart, depending on the variety.
- **Light Requirements:** Full sun

Special Care Notes:

Marigolds thrive in well-drained, slightly acidic soil. They are low-maintenance and need little water once established. Keep them deadheaded to encourage continuous blooming.

Harvesting

- **When to Harvest:** When flowers are fully open, typically in late spring to fall.
- **How to Harvest:** Cut flowers at the base of the stem, just above the foliage.
- **Storage Tips:** Dry marigold flowers or store them in a cool, dry place. They also make great additions to bouquets.

Pro Tips & Quirks

- Marigolds are great at repelling pests like aphids and nematodes, making them perfect for companion planting anywhere in the garden.
- **Common mistake:** Overwatering. Marigolds prefer drier conditions once established.

Friend: EVERYONE!

Foe: Give them space as they grow. They get quite large by fall and do best with space to bloom.

Zinnias

Difficulty Level: Easy

Best For: Gardeners who love bold, colorful flowers that attract pollinators. These are also spectacular as cut flowers. Some tips. When blooms are in full show, use a protecting netting to keep munching bugs away. Also, do a little stem shake to make sure it is firm and not wobbly and will hold up in a vase. I usually choose a color theme for the year just to please my own eyes so my favorite changes from year to year but I am a sucker for anything striped or two-toned. Pro tip: Save the seeds and you'll have a huge variety to choose from.

Favorite Varieties

- **Peppermint Stick:** Known for its large, vibrantly-striped flowers in a range of colors.
- **Queeny Lime:** Impressive and always stunning, this series of zinnias is a personal favorite for its green-tinged coral blooms.
- **Persian Carpet:** an honorable mention. I love this shorter variety that stuns with its burgundies and golds, mimicking marigolds in looks but with more variety and flare.

Growing Guide:

- **Birthday:** about 6-10 days from seed.
- **Days to Maturity:** 60-70 days
- **When to Start:** Start indoors 6-8 weeks before the last frost or sow directly outdoors once the soil has warmed up.
- **Special Spacing Requirements:** Space plants 6-12 inches apart, depending on the variety.
- **Light Requirements:** Full sun

Special Care Notes

Zinnias like well-drained, slightly acidic soil with good organic matter. They prefer consistent watering but need good air circulation to avoid fungal diseases.

Harvesting

- **When to Harvest:** When flowers are fully open and colorful.
- **How to Harvest:** Cut flowers in the morning when they're fully hydrated, and snip stems just above the leaf node.
- **Storage Tips:** Store cut flowers in a vase, or dry them by hanging them upside down.

Pro Tips & Quirks

- Zinnias attract pollinators like butterflies and bees, making them a great addition to your garden's ecosystem.
- **Common mistake:** Not giving enough space. Zinnias like room to grow, so make sure they have enough air circulation.

Sunflowers

Difficulty Level: Easy

Best For: Gardeners who want a dramatic, towering presence in their garden with the added benefit of edible seeds. Or choose a dwarf variety for a shorter bloom that still stuns.

Favorite Varieties

- **Mammoth:** These giants can grow up to 12 feet tall and produce large (yummy) seeds.
- **Teddy Bear:** A compact, double-flowered variety perfect for small spaces.

Growing Guide

- **Birthday:** about 7-10 days from seed.
- **Days to Maturity:** 70-90 days
- **When to Start:** Start seeds directly outdoors after the last frost date or sow indoors for an earlier start.
- **Special Spacing Requirements:** Space plants 12-18 inches apart for small varieties, or 18-24 inches for larger types.
- **Light Requirements:** Full sun

Special Care Notes

Sunflowers need well-drained, fertile soil with plenty of organic matter. They are drought-tolerant once established, but they require consistent watering during their growing season.

Harvesting

- **When to Harvest:** Harvest when the back of the sunflower head turns yellow and the seeds are plump and mature.
- **How to Harvest:** Cut the head with a few inches of stem attached.
- **Storage Tips:** Dry heads in a well-ventilated space. Once dry, rub the seeds out or store the whole head for easy access.

Pro Tips & Quirks

- Sunflowers are best planted where they'll get plenty of sunlight as they can grow quite tall and need support to stay upright.
- **Common mistake:** Not staking taller varieties. Sunflowers can be top-heavy and need support as they grow.

Friends: Just about everyone!

Foes: These guys leave a shadow. Make sure to plant partial shade loving plants in the same bed.

Gazania

Difficulty Level: Easy

Best For: Gardeners looking for vibrant, drought-tolerant flowers that grow low to the ground and add beauty to small spaces.

Favorite Varieties

- **Kiss:** Known for its vibrant colors and compact growth, perfect for containers.
- **Treasure:** Features large, showy flowers with unique patterns.

Growing Guide

- **Birthday:** about 14-21 days from seed.
- **Days to Maturity:** 60-70 days
- **When to Start:** Start indoors 6-8 weeks before the last frost, or sow directly outdoors once the soil has warmed up.
- **Special Spacing Requirements:** Space plants 8-12 inches apart.
- **Light Requirements:** FULL sun

Special Care Notes

Gazania thrives in a well-drained, sandy, or loamy soil. They're very drought-tolerant once established and need little watering once they're settled in.

Harvesting

- **When to Harvest:** Flowers are ready to be cut when fully open and bright.
- **How to Harvest:** Snip the stems near the base of the plant, cutting above a leaf node.
- **Storage Tips:** Gazanias are typically grown for their ornamental value, so they're best enjoyed fresh, but you can dry the flowers for decoration.

Pro Tips & Quirks

- Gazania's flowers close at night and during cloudy weather, so make sure you plant them in a spot with plenty of sun!
- **Common mistake:** Planting them in too much shade. Gazania thrives in full sun and can be temperamental if not given enough light.

Dahlia (Seed)

Difficulty Level: Intermediate

Best For: Gardeners looking for a stunning, high-impact flower with a bit more complexity in its care.

Dahlias are not the easiest flower to grow. They require attention to detail, particularly when it comes to spacing, watering, and managing tubers in the fall. However, their beauty and diversity make them worth the effort, and with a little experience, they'll reward you with breathtaking blooms. For those looking for a simpler (and less expensive) introduction to Dahlias, I recommend starting with dwarf seeds which skip the need for tubers and planting in the fall. These still offer a spectacular display in late summer but with a much cheaper price tag and if you are not desperate to know exactly what type of flower is coming up, then these seeds will suit you just fine. Some things we do for the sheer beauty of it. Dahlias are one of those things.

Favorite Variety

- **Cactus Flowered Blend:** These flowers come in a range of colors, from deep reds to soft pinks and yellows, with petals that curl and twist like cactus spines.

Growing Guide

- **Birthday:** 10-15 days from seed.
- **Days to Maturity:** 75-120 days (depending on conditions)
- **When to Start:** Start indoors in early spring, about 6-8 weeks before the last expected frost date. Transplant seedlings outdoors after the danger of frost has passed and the soil is warm.
- **Spacing Requirements:** Space plants 18-24 inches apart to allow for good airflow and room to grow.
- **Light Requirements:** Full sun (6-8 hours of direct sunlight per day).

Special Care Notes

- Dahlias thrive in well-drained, nutrient-rich soil. Be sure to amend the soil with compost or aged manure for optimal growth.
- Water regularly, especially during the flowering period, but avoid overhead watering to reduce the risk of mildew.
- During the fall, dig up the tubers before the first frost and store them in a cool, dry place over the winter to replant in spring.

Harvesting

- **When to Harvest:** Once blooms reach full size and show their characteristic "cactus" petal formation. This typically occurs in mid to late summer.
- **How to Harvest:** Use sharp scissors or pruners to cut the stems of dahlias just above the first set of leaves. For the best vase life, harvest flowers in the morning when they are still cool.
- **Storage Tips:** Dahlias are best enjoyed fresh, but if you're saving seeds, allow the flowers to dry on the plant before collecting seeds. Store saved seeds in a cool, dry place for the next growing season.

Pro Tips & Quirks

- **Common Mistake:** Overcrowding the plants. They need space to grow and thrive, so don't try to plant too many in one spot.
- Fun Fact: The world of dahlia collectors is a vibrant one, with some gardeners dedicating their entire collections to crossing and creating new varieties. It's a glorious, and occasionally crazy, world where passion for this flower knows no bounds!

While not an easy grower, these flowers are gorgeous and make me smile—once you're hooked on dahlias, there's no turning back! Once again, these flowers are great polinators and have few enemies.

Rosemary

Basil

Lamiacede

Lamiaceae family

These aromatic plants are beloved for their culinary and medicinal uses. With minimal effort, they thrive in gardens and containers, rewarding you with fragrant leaves and flowers.

Thyme

Lemon Balm

Oregano

LAMINACEAE

Herbs For Every Season

The Lamiaceae Family - Herbs That Transform Your Garden and Kitchen

- **Basil:** *Fragrant herb used in pesto, sauces, and salads.*
- **Lemon Balm:** *Citrus-scented herb great for teas and calming remedies.*
- **Rosemary:** *Aromatic herb perfect for roasting and savory dishes.*
- **Thyme:** *Earthy herb used in soups, meats, and marinades.*
- **Oregano:** *Robust herb ideal for pizza, pasta, and Mediterranean dishes.*
- **Wild & Wonderful:** *Wild Oregano: Bold, untamed flavor perfect for rustic culinary creations.*

The only family I consider to truly *thrive* in small containers is what I affectionately call the herb family. Officially known as the Lamiaceae family, it is full of aromatic wonders—herbs that bring flavor, fragrance, and a touch of elegance to your garden. These plants are well-loved for their versatility, from spicing up your cooking to offering medicinal benefits. They also have low nutrient demands, which makes them ideal for small spaces, large pots, and patio gardens.

Not all plants in the kingdom take to such a life with ease. Heavy feeders, such as fruit-producing plants, do not naturally thrive in containers. Typically too small, shallow, or unwieldy to be practical, these setups require significant augmentation for the plants to yield well.

If you're tight on space and want a guaranteed "wow" factor, stick with herbs. Bonus: many of these plants love to spread! Lemon balm and peppermint, for instance, are among the most aggressive growers. However, they make lovely teas and behave nicely when confined to pots. I recommend dotting your landscape with round containers to prevent an herbal takeover while still adding beauty to your garden.

Basil

Difficulty Level: Easy

Best For: Small spaces, beginning gardeners, and anyone who loves cooking with fresh herbs.

Favorite Varieties

- **Genovese:** Classic basil, perfect for pesto or fresh salads.
- **Sweet Thai:** A slightly spicier, more fragrant basil-ideal for Thai dishes and stir-fries.

Growing Guide

- **Birthday:** 5-7 days from seed.
- **Days to Maturity:** 60-90 days
- **When to Start:** Late spring, after the last frost
- **Special Spacing Requirements:** Space 10-12 inches apart for optimal growth.
- **Light Requirements:** Full sun

Special Care Notes

Basil loves warmth, so plant it only after the last frost. Without enough sunlight, it can become leggy, so keep it in a sunny spot.

Harvesting

- **When to Harvest:** Once the plant is at least 6 inches tall.
- **How to Harvest:** Pinch off leaves, cutting just above a set of leaves to encourage bushy growth.
- **Storage Tips:** Store basil in a jar of water or freeze it in ice cubes for long-term use.

Pro Tips & Quirks

- Basil thrives in warm temperatures, so keep it cozy.
- **Common mistake:** Not pinching off flowers—once basil flowers, it can become bitter and stop producing new leaves.

Friend: Great with tomatoes, oregano, and peppers.

Foe: Avoid planting near sage or rosemary, as they can compete for resources.

Lemon Balm

Difficulty Level: Easy

Best For: Small spaces, herb lovers, or anyone wanting a calming, fragrant herb.

Favorite Varieties:

- **All Varieties:** Known for its lemony fragrance and gentle flavor.

Growing Guide:

- **Birthday:** 7-14 days from seed.
- **Days to Maturity:** 70-90 days
- **When to Start:** Early spring
- **Special Spacing Requirements:** Space 12 inches apart for adequate air circulation.
- **Light Requirements:** Full sun to partial shade

Special Care Notes

Lemon balm loves to spread and can quickly take over a garden bed. Grow it in containers or designated areas to prevent it from crowding other plants.

Harvesting

- **When to Harvest:** 6-8 weeks after planting, when the leaves are lush and fragrant.
- **How to Harvest:** Snip leaves with scissors and use fresh for teas or salads.
- **Storage Tips:** Dried lemon balm can be stored in airtight containers for tea or medicinal use.

Pro Tips & Quirks

- Grows best in well-drained soil.
- **Common mistake:** Letting it go to seed without containmen—-it'll pop up everywhere.

Friend: Great with peppermint, chamomile, and thyme.

Foe: Can overwhelm nearby plants if not kept contained.

Oregano

Difficulty Level: Easy

Best For: Beginners and gardeners with limited space-this hardy herb thrives in containers and raised beds.

Favorite Varieties

- **Greek Oregano:** The classic variety, great for Mediterranean dishes.
- **Italian Oregano:** A milder, slightly sweeter flavor.

Growing Guide

- **Birthday:** about 7-14 days from seed.
- **Days to Maturity:** 80-90 days
- **When to Start:** Early spring, once the frost is gone
- **Special Spacing Requirements:** Space 12-18 inches apart for spreading.
- **Light Requirements:** Full sun

Special Care Notes

Oregano thrives in dry, well-drained soil and is drought-tolerant. Avoid overwatering.

Harvesting

- **When to Harvest:** 2-3 months after planting, once the leaves have a strong flavor.
- **How to Harvest:** Snip leaves, cutting just above a leaf node.
- **Storage Tips:** Dry oregano by hanging bunches upside down or using a dehydrator.

Pro Tips & Quirks

- Oregano can spread rapidly, so consider potting this one up.
- **Common mistake:** Overwatering. Oregano prefers dry conditions.

Friend: Pairs well with tomatoes, basil, and thyme.

Foe: Avoid planting next to mint as they will compete for space.

Rosemary & Sage

Difficulty Level: Easy

Best For: Perennial herb lovers and gardeners who enjoy flavorful, aromatic plants.

Favorite Varieties:

- **Rosemary:** Tuscan Blue-a hardy variety with fragrant, needle-like leaves, perfect for roasting meats.
- **Sage:** Purple Sage—a beautiful variety with purple leaves and a milder flavor.

Growing Guide

- **Birthday:** Sage- about 2-3 weeks; Rosemary- about 3-4 weeks.
- **Days to Maturity:** Rosemary, 90-120 days; Sage, 75-85 days
- **When to Start:** Early spring, after the last frost
- **Special Spacing Requirements:** Space rosemary 12-18 inches apart; sage 12 inches apart.
- **Light Requirements:** Full sun

Special Care Notes

Both rosemary and sage love dry, well-drained soil and are drought-tolerant. They thrive in full sun and can handle heat once established.

Harvesting

- **When to Harvest:** After the plant is established, typically in summer.
- **How to Harvest:** Trim sprigs as needed, cutting above a leaf node.
- **Storage Tips:** Dry by hanging or using a dehydrator.

Pro Tips & Quirks

- Both are perennials and will return year after year.
- **Common mistake:** Not giving enough space to grow—both need room to spread.

Friend: Pairs well with thyme, oregano, and lavender.

Foe: Avoid planting near basil as they can compete for space and nutrients.

Wild and Wonderful

Self-Heal (Prunella vulgaris)

- **Description:** This lovely little herb is found all over lawns and near forests and meadows Known for its wound-healing properties, it's a must-have for a backyard herbalist.

- **Uses:** Traditionally, Self-Heal has been used in teas, salves, and poultices for its anti-inflammatory and wound-healing properties. It's also edible perfect for salads or soups.

- **Growing Habit:** Self-heal spreads through rhizomes and can act as ground cover. You don't want to plant this intentionally, as it will take over, but if you're blessed enough to have it in your yard, enjoy it!

- **Friend:** Works well with other ground covers like clover and creeping thyme.

- **Foe:** Can be invasive in some areas if not kept in check.

Kale

Kale

Brassicacede

Brassicaceae Family

These nutrient-packed plants are staples in many gardens, known for their versatility and cool-season resilience. With proper care, they provide a steady supply of greens and roots.

Broccoli

Cauliflower

Cabbage

BRASSICACEAE

Bold and Beautiful

The Brassicaceae Family - Kale, Cabbage, and Beyond

- **Broccoli:** *Nutrient-packed veggie with crisp florets, perfect for steaming or roasting.*
- **Cauliflower:** *Versatile vegetable great for mashing, roasting, or making low-carb rice.*
- **Cabbage:** *Leafy head used in slaws, soups, and fermented dishes like sauerkraut.*
- **Kale:** *Hardy green for salads, smoothies, and sauteing; rich in vitamins.*
- **Radish:** *Crisp and peppery root, ideal for salads or quick pickling.*

General Characteristics: Known for their cancer-fighting properties, these antioxidant-rich plants are ideal for cool-season gardening. Whether you're growing leafy greens or root vegetables, members of the Brassicaceae family are versatile and provide a steady supply of nutritious crops.

Growing Conditions: They thrive in rich, well-drained soil with a slightly acidic to neutral pH (6.0 to 7.5). Adding compost or aged manure helps ensure healthy growth. Crop rotation is recommended to prevent soil-borne diseases.

Common Family Traits: These plants are adapted to cool-season growth and flourish in moderate temperatures. They tend to grow quickly, offering a consistent supply of greens and roots.

Friends & Foes (Family Level)

- **Friends:** Besides the popular herbs and marigolds, onions, garlic, kale, cabbage, and radishes are excellent companions. They support each other by deterring pests, boosting growth, and improving soil health.
- **Foes:** Avoid planting near strawberries, peppers, or tomatoes, as these plants can compete for nutrients and are susceptible to similar pests and diseases.

Planting Instructions

For new gardeners, especially those in the Northeast, the fear of frost is real. But the good news is that many brassicas can handle a light frost, and for gardeners in the cooler parts of Zone 5, this opens up an exciting opportunity! Here's how to know when it's safe to plant:

- **Zone 5:** Plant out brassicas **3-4 weeks before the last expected frost** (typically early May, depending on your frost dates). Ensure the ground is not frozen solid, and that your plants have been properly "hardened off" (this means gradually acclimating your plants to outdoor conditions by placing them outside during the day but bringing them in at night for 1-2 weeks). If purchasing starts, ask the grower if the plants are hardened off.
- **Zones 6-7:** Plant out brassicas **4-6 weeks before the last expected frost,** generally **mid to late March for Zone** 7 and **late April to early May for Zone 6.** Don't forget to harden off your plants!

Special Considerations
- Brassicaceae plants can tolerate frost and often thrive in cooler weather, growing well into late fall. These make great season extenders because you can get an early and late crop by succession planting.
- Ensure consistent moisture for optimal growth, especially during germination and early growth stages.

Arugula

Difficulty Level: Easy

Best For: Small spaces, beginning gardeners, or anyone craving fast-growing greens.

Favorite Varieties
- **Wild Rocket:** A peppery, slightly bitter flavor, ideal for salads and garnishes.
- **Astro:** A milder variety with tender leaves, perfect for salad mixes.

Growing Guide
- **Birthday:** about 7-10 days from seed.
- **Days to Maturity:** 40-50 days
- **When to Start:** Early spring or fall
- **Special Spacing Requirements:** Space 6 inches apart in rows for optimal growth.
- **Light Requirements:** Full sun to partial shade

Special Care Notes

Arugula loves cool weather and isn't a fan of heat. Plant it early in the spring or late in the fall, and pull the plants out completely by the end of June to avoid the dreaded bolting (when it goes to seed and grows flowers).

Harvesting

- **When to Harvest:** 4-6 weeks after planting when the leaves are large enough to pick.
- **How to Harvest:** Harvest the outer leaves first, letting the center continue growing.
- **Storage tips:** Store in the fridge for up to a week. Can be used fresh or in cooking.

Pro Tips & Quirks

- **Common mistake:** Not spacing plants enough can lead to smaller, crowded leaves.
- **Bonus tip:** If arugula does go to seed, embrace it—you can enjoy the peppery greens forever.

Friend: Great companions for radishes, carrots, and peas.

Foe: Avoid planting with tomatoes or peppers.

Cauliflower

Member: Broccoli/Cauliflower

Difficulty Level: Moderate

Best For: Cool-Season gardeners or those with a little more space.

Favorite Varieties

- **Calabrcse:** Classic, large-flowered broccoli with rich, green heads.
- **Snowball:** A compact cauliflower with tight, white heads.

Growing Guide

- **Birthday:** about 8-14 days from seed.
- **Days to Maturity:** 50-85 days

- **When to Start:** Start indoors 6-8 weeks before the last frost, then transplant.
- **Special Spacing Requirements:** Space 18-24 inches apart for both broccoli and cauliflower.
- **Light Requirements:** Full sun

Special Care Notes:

Consistent moisture is crucial, especially during head formation. They may require a little extra fertilizer, especially during the growing season.

Harvesting

- **When to Harvest:** When heads are firm and tight before they start to flower.
- **How to harvest:** Cut the head off with a sharp knife, leaving some stalk.
- **Storage tips:** Best eaten fresh but can be stored in the fridge for 1-2 weeks.

Pro Tips & Quirks

- Cauliflower is more temperature-sensitive than broccoli. Avoid hot weather to prevent poor head development.
- **Common mistake:** Letting the heads grow too large or delaying harvesting, causing them to open up into flowers.
- **Confession:** I rarely grow these, not because they are difficult, but because they are space hogs and a low return for our large family. I would have to grow *so much* cauliflower or broccoli to make a dent in our family's veggie intake.
- **Friend:** Great companions for onions, garlic, and beets.

Cabbage

Difficulty Level: Moderate

Best For: Cool-season crops or anyone with space to grow heads of cabbage.

Favorite Varieties

- **Savoy:** Wrinkled leaves, excellent for both raw and cooked dishes. Key player in Kimchi.
- **Green Copenhagen:** A classic, compact head that's perfect for coleslaw and stir-fries.

Growing Guide

- **Birthday:** about 7-14 days from seed.
- **Days to Maturity:** 70-100 days
- **When to Start:** 6-8 weeks before the last frost indoors, then transplant.
- **Special Spacing Requirements:** Space 18-24 inches apart.
- **Light Requirements:** Full sun

Special Care Notes

Water regularly to keep the soil moist, especially as the heads start to form.

Harvesting

- **When to Harvest:** When the heads feel firm and solid.
- **How to Harvest:** Cut off the entire head at the base.
- **Storage tips:** Can be stored in a cool, dark place for several weeks. We love fermented sauerkraut. It is super easy—just salt and cabbage.

Pro Tips & Quirks

- **Common mistake:** Not spacing cabbage properly, leading to smaller heads.
- Cabbage needs time and space to grow-it's not ideal for raised beds since it can monopolize prime real estate for much of the growing season, but it's still doable if you are determined.
- Cabbage loves cool weather, so plant early to avoid bolting when the heat kicks in or plant late July for a fall harvest. Keep well watered.

Friend: Works well with kale, onions, and beets.

Foe: Dill releases a compound that interferes with cabbage growth. Peppers and tomatoes are nutrient-hungry like cabbage and compete for soil food. Beans are on the fence, as the nitrogen-fixing properties don't really benefit cabbage but I don't notice an negative impact.

Kale

Difficulty Level: Easy

Best For: Beginning gardeners or those wanting leafy greens year-round.

Favorite Varieties

- **Curly Kale:** Classic variety, perfect for salads or smoothies.
- **Lacinato (Dinosaur Kale):** A flatter, darker leaf with a mild flavor.

Growing Guide

- **Birthday:** about 5-8 days from seed.
- **Days to Maturity:** 50-75 days
- **When to Start:** Early spring or late summer for fall crops.
- **Special Spacing Requirements:** Space 12-18 inches apart.
- **Light Requirements:** Full sun to partial shade

Special Care Notes:

Kale can tolerate some frost, making it perfect for cooler months. Water consistently, especially during the warm months, to prevent leaves from becoming tough.

Harvesting

- **When to Harvest:** When leaves are large enough to eat but before they get too tough.
- **How to Harvest:** Snip leaves from the outside of the plant.
- **Storage tips:** Keep in the fridge for up to a week.

Pro Tips & Quirks

- Kale is frost-tolerant, which can improve its flavor.
- One kale plant can last an entire summer! Harvest the outer leaves and let the center continue to grow. Cabbage worms LOVE kale. Soak leaves in salt water to loosen bugs before cooking. We've had many a time when a less-than-stellar wash revealed a bug on our dinner plate.
- **Common mistake:** Not harvesting the leaves young enough—older leaves can become bitter.

Friend: Great with most veggies. Nourish well with compost if planted with nitrogen-hungry plants like tomatoes and peppers.

Foe: Flea beetles and cabbage moths love these leaves so avoid planting with cabbage, broccoli, or other plants that attract those same pests.

Radish

Difficulty Level: Easy

Best For: Small space gardeners or those wanting quick results.

Favorite Varieties

- **Cherry Belle:** The classic red radish, great for salads.
- **Daikon:** A larger, milder variety, perfect for pickling or stir fry.

Growing Guide

- **Birthday:** about 5 days from seed.
- **Days to Maturity:** 20-30 days
- **When to Start:** Early spring or fall
- **Special Spacing Requirements:** Space 2 inches apart for small radishes, or 4 inches for larger varieties.
- **Light Requirements:** Full sun

Special Care Notes

Radishes grow quickly but can become woody or spicy if left too long.

Harvesting

- **When to Harvest:** When roots are firm and the size you want.
- **How to harvest:** Gently pull the radish from the soil.
- **Storage tips:** Store in the fridge for up to 2 weeks.

Pro Tips & Quirks

Common mistake: Leaving radishes in the ground too long, causing them to become bitter and woody.

Friend: Best paired with peas, lettuce, or carrots.

Foe: Vining plants like melons, cucumbers, zucchini will shade out raishes and carrots will compete in the root zone. To get around that, plant nearby early in the season when the plants are small. Cabbages are not super-friendly and just attract a lot of pests that do not allow radishes to thrive.

Green Beans

Fabacede

Fabaceae Family

Known as the legume family, these plants are prized for their ability to improve soil fertility while producing delicious and nutritious crops. With their nitrogen-fixing roots, they're a gardener's best friend.

Dry beans

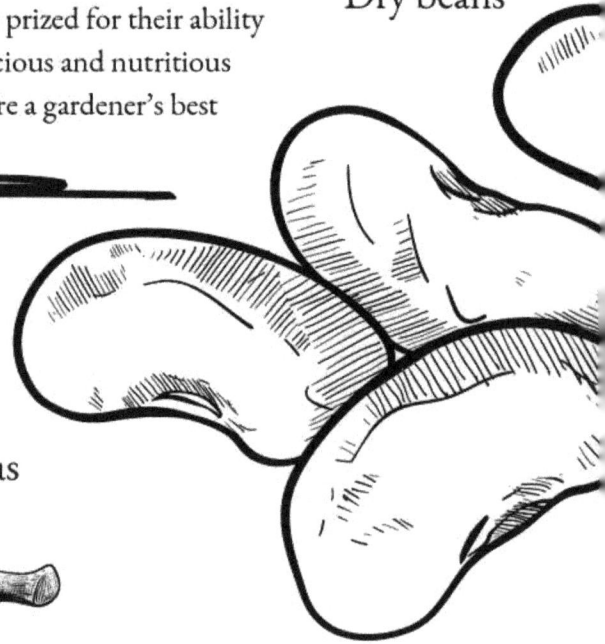

Sweet Peas

FABACEAE

Beans and Sweet Peas for Every Space

Peas (Snap, Snow, Shell): *Sweet spring climbers that enrich the soil with nitrogen.*
Green Beans (Bush & Pole): *Versatile producers-bush types for quick harvests, pole types for season-long picking.*
Dry Beans *(Black, Pinto, Kidney}: Low-maintenance protein powerhouses that store well for years when properly dried.*

General Characteristics

The Fabaceae family is like the best friend every garden need—these plants are natural soil enhancers! They fix nitrogen into the soil, improving its fertility while producing nutrient-packed crops. If you're into sustainable gardening, these are your go-to plants. They do the heavy lifting for your soil, reducing your need for fertilizer.

Growing Conditions

Fabaceae plants prefer well-drained soil with some organic matter—think compost or aged manure. They like slightly acidic to neutral soil (pH 6.0 to 7.0). Give them a sunny spot, and they'll thrive.

Common Family Traits

- Warm-weather lovers (though peas enjoy cooler temperatures).
- Great companions for a variety of crops (hello, nitrogen boost!).
- Easy to grow, perfect for gardeners looking for high-yielding, low-maintenance plants.

Friends: These plants love hanging out with beans (green, Calypso, pinto), peas, carrots, cucumbers, and corn. They promote healthy growth and help keep pests at bay.

Foes: Watch out for tomatoes, onions, garlic, and fennel—they're not the best neighbors for Fabaceae plants. These can compete for nutrients and cause some garden tension.

Special Considerations
- Since Fabaceae plants are nitrogen fixers, you don't need to fertilize them as often, but be cautious of planting them near heavy feeders that rely on nitrogen.
- Compost old plant material for a soil boost—it's a win for your garden's future health. Remember that stored nitrogen is released when the plant breaks down.
- Fabaceae plants love good drainage so don't let them sit in soggy soil.

Sweet Peas

Difficulty Level: Easy

Best For: Gardeners who are just starting out or those with small garden spaces. Sweet peas love cool weather, so they're a great pick for early spring planting!

Favorite Varieties
- **Sugar Snap:** Sweet and crisp, these are the peas you can't stop snacking on right off the vine.
- **Snow Peas:** Flat and tender, these peas are a stir-fry's best friend and are perfect for salads too.

Growing Guide
- **Birthday:** about 10 days from seed.
- Start from seed.
- Sprouts in 7-10 days.
- **Spacing Requirements:** Plant in pairs to ensure germination, 1 inch deep. Space bush peas 1-2 inches apart. For vining varieties, space them 3-4 inches apart. Space rows 2 feet apart. NOTE: Peas are quite forgiving on spacing. I love having kids help plant because they are large seeds and still do amazing if sown less than precisely.
- **Days to Maturity:** 60-70 days
- **When to Start:** Early spring, about 4-6 weeks before your last frost date.
- **Light Requirements:** Full sun, but if you're in a hot climate, they'll appreciate a little afternoon shade.

Special Care Notes
Peas prefer cooler weather, so make sure you start them early. Water consistently, but avoid soggy soil, or you'll risk root rot.

Harvesting

- When to Harvest: Peas are ready when the pods are plump, but before they start to wrinkle. If they get too old, they lose that sweet snap and start tasting more "woody."
- How to Harvest: Gently pull the pods from the vines. The younger the sweeter so don't let them languish on the vine.
- Storage Tips: Keep fresh peas in the fridge for up to a week, or freeze them for long-term storage.

Pro Tips & Quirks

- Peas LOVE climbing, so give them a trellis or support system. They'll be happier and you'll be able to collect more beans.
- **Common mistake:** Overwatering. Too much moisture can cause root rot, so make sure your soil drains well.

Friend: Peas love carrots, radishes, cucumbers, and corn. They'll help their neighbors thrive while fixing nitrogen in the soil.

Foe: Alliums release a compound that can slow pea growth—give plenty of space. Space 3-4 feet apart. Even better, put a barrier crop between them. Fennel also releases chemicals that inhibit the growth. Tomatoes, peppers and eggplants don't like to be too close.

WHAT IS INOCULATION?

Beans and peas are part of the legume family, which can "fix" nitrogen in the soil with the help of special bacteria. These bacteria (Rhizobia) form a partnership with the plants, creating little nitrogen-packed nodules on their roots. This gives your plants a natural fertilizer boost and improves soil health for the next planting. Inoculation makes sure that the correct bacteria is in your soil. This is optional, but it's a small, organic step to supercharge your legume crops!

How to Inoculate (the Organic Way):

1. Choose Organic Inoculant: Look for a Rhizobium-based organic inoculant labeled for beans and peas. It's usually a powder.

2. Dampen Seeds: Moisten your seeds lightly with water so the inoculant sticks.

3. Dust with Inoculant: Sprinkle or roll the seeds in the powder until they're lightly coated.

4. Plant Right Away: Sow the seeds in well-drained soil as soon as they're inoculated.

Tips for Success:

- Rotate Crops: Don't grow beans and peas in the same spot every year. This will help prevent soil imbalances.

- Improve Soil: Use organic compost to give the bacteria a healthy environment to thrive.

- Only Once: You don't need to inoculate if you've grown legumes in that spot recently, as the bacteria will already be there.

Green Beans

(Bush and Pole Varieties)

Difficulty Level: Easy

Best For: Beginning gardeners or those working with limited space. Bush beans are particularly great for small gardens, while pole beans are perfect for vertical gardening.

Favorite Varieties

- **Tavara:** These French fillet beans are thin, tender, and produce well—ideal for fresh eating.

- **Provider:** A hearty bean, perfect for preserving or eating fresh. These beans hold up well and stay tender when picked young.

Growing Guide

- **Birthday:** about 7-10 days from seed.

- **Days to Harvest:** 50-60 days for bush beans

- **When to Start:** Late spring, after the last frost, once the soil is warm.

- **Spacing Requirements:** For bush beans, space 4-6 inches apart. For pole beans, space them 6-12 inches apart and provide vertical support for climbing.

- **Light Requirements:** Full sun—beans love warmth and sunshine!

Special Care Notes: Beans perform best in temperatures between 70°F and 85°F (21°C to 29°C), so be sure to wait for those warm days. Consistent watering is important, especially during pod development, but be careful not to overdo it—moist roots can lead to trouble.

Harvesting

- **When to Harvest:** Pick when the pods are firm and fully formed, but before they start getting too mature and stringy.
- **How to Harvest:** Snap beans off the stem by hand. Tavera is a dreamy experience of tender thin beans that are scrumptious in the 4-6 inch range. Pick every other day at the peak and make sure that little fingers are gentle and don't snap branches when picking.
- **Storage Tips:** Beans can be stored in a cool, dry place or frozen for long-term storage.

Pro Tips & Quirks

- Bush beans are perfect for small spaces—no trellis needed. But if you're growing pole beans, make sure they have a structure to climb.
- Hilling (mounding soil around the plant) adds support to even bush beans, which do a little better with the help. Soils rich in potassium and phosphorus won't need this extra push but better safe than sorry—hill the beans at 3 weeks old. Blossoms should begin in a week or two and shortly after that you'll be ready to harvest.
- Common mistake: Not giving pole beans enough support. Without a trellis, they'll sprawl rather than climb!

Friend: Best companions: Beans love corn, cucumbers, and radishes. They help improve soil quality by fixing nitrogen, benefiting their companions.

Foe: Alliums and Fennel can inhibit growth similar to peas. Give 3-4 feet of space and plant a barrier crop between. Tomatoes, peppers and eggplants compete for nutrients, so avoid pairing these or plan on feeding intensively.

Dry Bean

Difficulty Level: Easy to Moderate

Best For: Gardeners looking to try something fun and different. This is what I call a "for the kids" grow. You are not going to grow enough dry beans to really make a huge impact in a small space. But you will grow some fun memories and the kids LOVE them.

Favorite Variety

- **Calypso Beans (aka Orea Beans):** These beans are small, round, and show off a unique black-and-white color pattern that makes them look more like a work of art than a legume. They're perfect for salads or soups. They look and taste like pinto beans when cooked.

Growing Guide

- **Birthday: about** 6-10 days from seed.
- **Days to Maturity:** 70-90 days
- **When to Start:** Direct sow outdoors once the soil warms up after the last frost. These beans love warm weather and need plenty of sun to grow strong.
- **Spacing Requirements:** Space seeds about 3 inches apart to give them room to spread out.
- **Light Requirements:** Full sun, as these beans are heat-loving and need at least 6 hours of sunlight a day.
- **Special Care Notes:** Calypso beans aren't too fussy, but they do like well-drained soil that's rich in organic matter. If you're starting them from seed, make sure you water them consistently until they're established, and then they'll take care of themselves.

Harvesting

- **When to Harvest:** These beans are ready for harvest when the pods are dry and brittle. If you're not sure, give them a little squeeze—if they make a popping sound, they're good to go.
- **How to Harvest:** Gently pull the pods from the vine. Let them dry completely before removing the beans from the pods.
- **Storage Tips:** Store dried beans in an airtight container in a cool, dark place. They can last for months this way.

Pro Tips & Quirks

- **Pro Tip:** Calypso beans are not only beautiful, but they're also great at fixing nitrogen in the soil, meaning they can actually help improve soil quality for other plants in the garden. Talk about a win-win!

- **Fun Fact:** They're sometimes called Orca beans because their color pattern resembles the black and white markings of orcas (killer whales). Kids LOVE these beans. When fresh, they are sweet and tasty. When dry, they are creamy and similar to a pinto bean.

- **Common Mistake:** Harvesting too soon. Let those pods dry on the vine for the best flavor and storage.

Friend and Foes: Same as green beans. Since these are going to stay put the whole growing season I recommend putting them in the center of the bed or at the end of your garden where their plain, drying stalks can be hidden better.

melons

winter squash

Cucurbitaceae

Sprawling Wonders

Cucumber

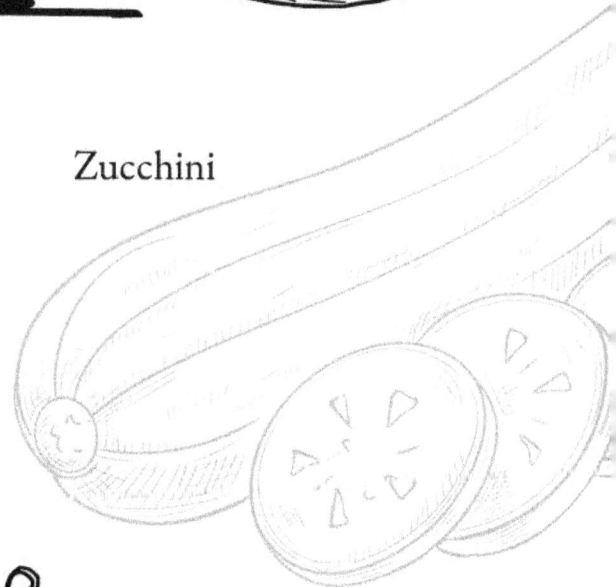

Zucchini

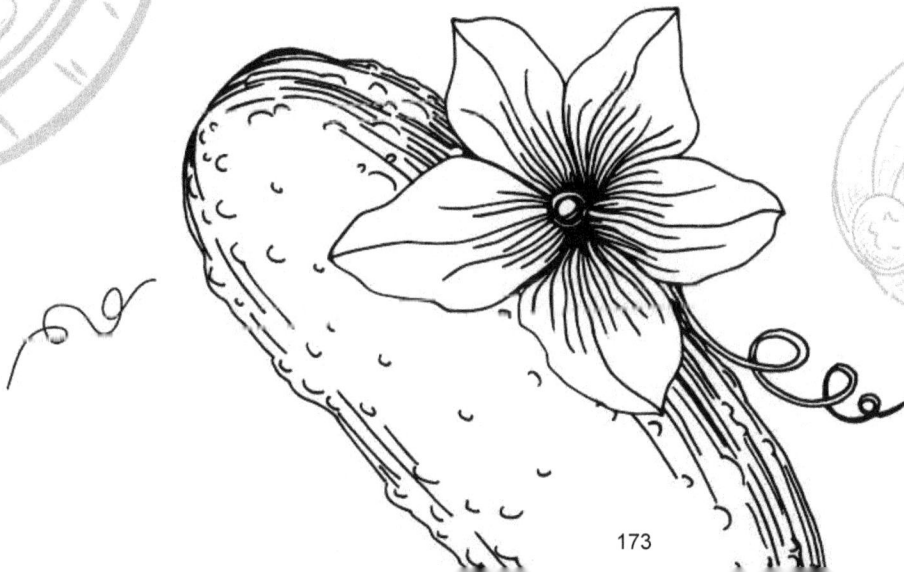

CUCURBITACEAE

Sprawling Wonders

Cucumbers: *Crisp, refreshing climbers perfect for slicing, pickling, or snacking.*

Melons: *Sweet, juicy fruits that bring summer flavor to every bite.*

Zucchini: *Prolific summer squash, great for grilling, baking, or spiralizing.*

Winter Squash: *Hardy, long-lasting varieties ideal for roasting and hearty soups.*

General Characteristics: Sprawling vines and bountiful fruit are the hallmarks of this family. From cucumbers to squash, melons to zucchini, these plants thrive in warmth and provide bountiful harvests. Whether you're growing summer squash like zucchini or the iconic cucumbers for pickling, this family offers a little something for every garden. Look for bush varieties. With space-saving techniques like trellising, you can make these sprawling wonders work for you. I highly recommend training to a cattle panel trellis if you plan to grow in a 4x8 bed.

Growing Conditions: These guys like it warm and breezy. If planted too close together or if watered in the evening, powdery mildew can wipe out your crops. Aphids also love these plants and you will want to keep a close eye on them.

Common Family Traits

> **Sprawling Growth:** These plants love to spread out. It's part of what makes them so prolific but also why they can take over a space quickly.
>
> **Prolific Producers:** While melons may require a bit more attention and a longer growing season, cucumbers and squash can churn out plenty of produce.
>
> **Trellising:** A great way to save space. Once these plants hit about 2 feet high, start training them up a fence or trellis to keep things tidy and make harvesting easier.

Friends: All flowers. These plants need pollinators to thrive. Herbs like basil, oregano, and parsley help to ward off pests naturally. Marigolds are another great option to keep aphids and other pests at bay. Dill is a maybe friend. Cucumbers are moody and sometimes they just don't thrive with the chemical dill releases in the soil. Give them space just to be safe. Think of it this way: they can sit at the same table just don't put them next to each other. Also they love working together when it comes time to eat, though! Cucumber and dill is a sensational flavor combo.

Foes: Solaneacea Family has a bit of a feud between these two. Maybe its because more people hold the pickles than ketchup on burgers—but either way, they don't like each other.

Pest and Problems

- **Aphids:** These tiny pests love to feed on cucumbers, melons, and squash. Keep an eye on the undersides of leaves, as aphids often congregate there.
- **Powdery Mildew:** A common issue for cucurbits, this fungal disease thrives in warm, humid conditions and can spread quickly.
- **Cucumber Beetles:** These pests can cause major damage to cucumbers and melons. Keep them in check by using row covers or soapy water. You can use an official insecticidal soap but I find dish soap works fine.

Special Considerations

- **Trellising:** As mentioned, once your squash or cucumbers reach about 2 feet high, it's time to start loosely securing them to a fence or trellis. This allows them to grow vertically, freeing up more space on the ground for other plants and improving airflow to prevent mildew. Plus, it keeps your fruits off the ground, reducing the risk of disease and pests.
- **Watering:** Always water at the base of the plants, keeping the leaves dry to prevent fungal issues. Early morning watering is best to allow the plant to dry out before evening.
- **Mulching:** Avoid heavy mulching around cucurbits, as they prefer their soil to dry out between waterings. Too much moisture can attract pests and fungal issues.

With the right care, members of the Cucurbitaceae family can be incredibly rewarding. Keep them well-spaced, watered, and trellised, and you'll be set for a summer full of delicious homegrown produce!

Cucumbers

Favorite Varieties

- **Spacemaster 80 Cucumber:** Perfect for tight spaces, this compact slicer delivers the crisp, fresh flavor you want without taking up a ton of garden real estate. It's a real game-changer for small-space gardeners!

- **Little Leaf Cucumber:** This variety is a compact climber, making it ideal for vertical gardening. Perfect for those tight corners or smaller spaces, it'll keep growing upwards instead of sprawling out, which is a huge win if you're working with limited space.

Growing Guide

- **Birthday:** 6-10 days from seed.

- **When to Start:** Cucumbers love warmth, so make sure you're starting them when temperatures are consistently above 60°F at night. You can either sow seeds directly in the soil once it's warmed up or start indoors to protect them from the cold and give them a head start.

- **Planting:** Once your seeds or transplants are ready, plant 2-4 seeds per hole, spacing them 24 inches apart. You'll want to give them plenty of room to spread out and grow. If you're using a trellis, place them 6 inches from the base to allow them to climb freely.

- **Pollination:** Cucumbers need a little help in the pollination department, so make sure to have plenty of flowers nearby to attract pollinators. This will ensure your plants aren't left to do the work themselves, and you'll see more fruit come harvest time.

Care Tips

- **Training to Fence (4 weeks):** Start training your cucumbers to grow up a trellis about 4 weeks after planting. This keeps them off the ground, reduces mildew, and helps you save space. Cucumbers are natural climbers and will appreciate the opportunity to reach for the sky!

- **Side-dress at 8 Weeks:** Cucumbers are heavy feeders, so around 8 weeks, give them a sidedress of rabbit manure, bone meal, and wood ash to keep the nitrogen levels high. This will help them produce those delicious fruits you're after.

- **Watering & Mulching:** Avoid mulching. Cucucurbits don't like their roots staying too damp overnight, which can lead to disease. Let them dry out in the evening for better results.

Harvesting

- **When to Harvest:** You'll typically be ready to harvest cucumbers about 10 weeks after planting. Aim to pick them when they're firm, shiny, and the right size for slicing-usually around 6-8 inches long. Keep an eye on them, as they can grow quickly!
- **How to Harvest:** Gently cut cucumbers from the vine, being careful not to damage the plant. They'll often slip right off when they're ready.

Pro Tips & Quirks:

- **Pro Tip:** Train those vines! Cucumbers love to climb. Giving them a vertical space to do so will save you a lot of room while keeping them healthier. Plus, it's fun to watch them grow!
- **Fun Fact:** Cucumbers grow fast—blink, and you might find you have a giant on your hands. It's a good idea to check them daily to get them at the perfect size for harvesting.
- **Common Mistake:** Don't wait too long to harvest—overripe cucumbers can turn soft and bitter. Get them when they're just right for the best flavor and texture.

Friends: Cucumbers get along with quite a few garden neighbors, especially those that bring in helpful bugs or keep pests in check. Cucumbers need pollinators to form fruit so fragrent herbs like **basil, oregano,** and **parsley** are good company as they are low-growing and won't crowd cucumbers. Flowers also attract pollinators and are perfectly paired here.

Marigolds are another solid pick. Their bold blooms aren't just for looks—they can help deter some of the bugs that love to munch on cucumber leaves.

Then there's **dill,** which is kind of the loud cousin at the party. It's great for attracting pollinators and beneficial insects but it grows fast and tall. If you plant dill nearby, give it its own corner so it doesn't throw shade (literally) on your cucumbers.

Foes: While cucumbers play nice with a lot of plants, there's one whole crew they'd rather avoid: the **Solanaceae** family-that's your **tomatoes, peppers, eggplant, and potatoes.** They might seem like they'd get along (after all, they're all warm-weather lovers), but they actually compete for similar nutrients and are prone to some of the same diseases, especially blights and wilts. Planting **cucumbers** near these heavy hitters can lead to stressed-out vines and a higher risk of trouble. Give each group their own space and keep the cucumbers with their calmer, friendlier companions instead.

Summer Squash

Favorite Varieties

- **Smooth Operator Yellow Squash:** This one is the quintessential garden squash—reliable, tender, and perfect for everything from stir-fry to roasting. It's the kind of squash that makes you feel like a garden pro with minimal fuss. It's a bush variety, meaning you can squeeze one plant into a 4x8 bed.
- **Green Squash-Black Beauty:** Black Beauty squash has that hearty, rich flavor that pairs so well with just about anything. Plus, it's versatile enough to work in savory dishes or even be turned into fritters. You get size without compromising on flavor—what's not to love?
- **Striped-Cocozelle:** If you're craving tender, zucchini-like squash without the overgrown monsters, Cocozelle is the way to go. Harvesting them when they're around 2 inches around and 6 inches long gives you that perfect tender texture.

Growing Guide

- **Birthday:** about 5-10 days from seed.
- **When to Start:** Aim for May 20th to start your seedlings. You'll want to give them a good jump start before the heat kicks in but *too* early, they might get leggy indoors. Timing is everything!
- **Planting:** Once your seedlings are ready, plant 2-4 on 8-inch high hills spaced 48 inches apart. You want them to have room to spread their roots out, but not so much room that they're competing with your other crops for space.
- **Pollination:** Here's where your flowers come into play. Pollination is key, and you want to let nature do its thing. Plant flowers nearby to attract pollinators and you'll avoid having to play matchmaker for your squash.

Harvesting

- **When to Harvest:** Aim to harvest when your squash is around 2 inches wide and 6 inches long. That's the sweet spot for tenderness and flavor.
- **How to Harvest:** Gently cut the squash from the vine when they reach that perfect size.
- **Storage Tips:** Store your squash in a cool, dry place, like your fridge or grate and freeze so you can have zucchini bread—or a nutrition boost for your soups all year long.

Pro Tips & Quirks

- **Pro Tip:** Keep flowers close by. It may seem like a simple tip, but it makes all the difference. Pollinators love those flowers and you'll be rewarded with a bountiful harvest.
- **Fun Fact:** Squash grow fast—blink, and you'll find a perfectly sized squash turning into something that might require a wheelbarrow to move. Keep an eye on them so you can enjoy the tender, flavorful ones before they get too big.
- **Common Mistake:** Don't wait too long to harvest. They turn into watery, flavorless giants. Smaller squash is the way to go—tender, sweet, and perfect every time.

Friends: Summer squash isn't too picky, but it definitely benefits from having the right neighbors. **Beans** are a top pick—they help improve the soil by fixing nitrogen, which squash loves. **Corn** can also be helpful, especially for smaller or bush varieties of squash. It grows tall and provides some light shade and support without crowding the base. **Nasturtiums** add a splash of color while helping to keep pests like aphids and squash bugs away. They're the kind of friend that looks good and pulls their weight. **Radishes** are another quiet helper—plant them early around your squash to confuse and deter pests like squash vine borers.

Foes: There are a few plants that don't play nicely with summer squash. **Cucumbers** might seem like they'd get along, but they attract a lot of the same pests and diseases, which just increases the risk for both. **Potatoes** are another poor match—they compete for nutrients, and both crops like to sprawl, which can quickly turn into a crowded mess. And while it might sound odd, even planting **zucchini** too close to other squash can backfire. They're both fast-growing and need room to breathe. If they're jammed together, airflow drops and diseases like powdery mildew can take hold. Give them elbow room, and they'll thank you with better harvests.

Mellons

If you have grown large mellons in Zones 5-6, I salute you. We have only been able to enjoy baby mellons. They are definitely a labor of love because they require so much space and offer small returns. Mellons are something we grow to delight our youngest gardeners. My top choices are from High Mowing Seeds.

Favorite Varieties

- **Black Mountain Watermellon**—a small, earlier-than-most, baby watermelon that thrives in short season climates, both cooler and hot/humid. This one is a winner, two hands raised.
- **PMR Delilcious S1 Mellon**—it's the higher yields and powdery mildew resistance that gets me. Dark orange fruit and sweet flavor.

Growing Guide

- **Birthday:** about 7-10 days from seed.
- **Days to Maturity:** 70-90 days
- **When to Start:** Direct sow outdoors once the soil warms up after the last frost. These beans love warm weather and need plenty of sun to grow strong.
- **Spacing Requirements:** Space seeds about 12-18 inches apart and only one row by your cattle panel trellis in a 4x8. If you are planting in the ground, space rows 6 feet apart.
- **Light Requirements:** Full sun, as these beans are heat-loving and need at least 8 hours of sunlight a day.

Special Care Notes

Mellons need warmth, good airflow and extra nutrition. Wood ash helps prevent blossom end rot by boosting calcium. Trace minerals needed to thrive—add compost.

Harvesting

- **When to Harvest:** This is the million-dollar question as there are hundreds of tips on how to tell when ripe. While many will have you thumping and smelling and doing all kinds of things, this is the simplest tip: Mark the calendar for suspected harvest date based on when you planted. Then check the leaf closest to the fruit. When it shrivels—it's time.
- **How to Harvest:** Gently cut mellon from the vine. Some varieties will naturally slip off when ripe. **Storage Tips:** Mellons can last for up to 4 weeks in the fridge after harvest!

Pro Tips & Quirks

- **Pro Tip:** Let them breathe. Kinda like an oldest child. These guys need their space.
- **Fun Fact:** You can save mellon seeds!
- **Common Mistake:** Harvesting too soon. Underripe mellons are no fun. Give them space.

Friends: Melons love the sun, warmth, and a little help from their garden neighbors. **Corn** can act as a living trellis for smaller melon varieties, offering gentle vertical support without crowding their roots. **Beans** bring the bonus of nitrogen-fixing, feeding the soil in a way melons appreciate. **Nasturtiums** earn their keep by attracting pollinators and distracting pests like aphids and squash bugs. They look cheerful doing it, too. **Radishes,** quick to grow and low-maintenance, help deter soil-dwelling pests and can be tucked around melon plants early in the season.

Foes: Melons have a few tricky relationships in the garden. Like most family members, shared vices mean **Cucumbers,** and other sprawling cousins, attract the same pests — and problems like powdery mildew and cucumber beetles. **Potatoes** are heavy feeders and compete with melons for nutrients and space, making both plants work harder than they should need to. And while **carrots** might seem harmless, their deep taproots can interfere with melon roots and may even slow melon growth if planted too close. Give melons room, good airflow, and friendly neighbors, and they'll reward you with sweet, sun-ripened fruit.

Winter Squash Guide

Favorite Varieties:

- **Waltham Butternut:** A classic, large butternut squash with sweet, nutty flavor.
- **Honey Nut:** Small, sweet squash perfect for 1-2 people.
- **Spaghetti Squash:** Requires ample space; yields fruit that has "strands" resembling spaghetti when cooked.
- **Delicata Bush:** Compact, bush-type squash ideal for raised beds.

Growing Guide

- **Birthday:** about 7-10 days fom seed.
- **Planting:** Start from seed or purchase transplants. Transplanting allows squash to be ready when harvesting garlic or onions mid-summer.
- **Spacing:** Provide ample space for sprawling vines; most full-size winter squash varieties need plenty of space. Look for bush or compact varieties.
- **Soil:** Plant in well-drained, fertile soil rich in organic matter. Start with nutrient rich soil. These are heavy feeders and need optimal nutrition the whole season.

- **Light:** Full sun is essential for optimal growth.
- **Watering:** Regular watering is crucial, especially during fruit development.

Harvesting
- **Timing:** Harvest when the skin is hard and the stem is dry.
- **Method:** Cut squash from the vine, leaving a 2-inch stem attached.
- **Storage:** Cure squash (skin thickens and hardens for winter storage) in a warm, dry place for 10-14 days before storing it in a cool, dry area.

Pro Tips & Quirks
- **Pro Tip:** Transplanting winter squash can lead to earlier harvests, aligning with the end of garlic or onion season.
- **Common Mistake:** Overcrowding plants; ensure adequate space for vines to spread.

Friends: Winter squash is a sprawling, heavy feeder, but it does well with a few strategic companions. **Beans** are a classic partner—they help fix nitrogen in the soil, giving winter squash a bit of a nutritional lift over time. **Corn** offers height and structure, and in a Three Sisters-style setup, squash helps shade the ground while corn rises above. **Marigolds** and **Nasturtiums** both pull double duty—adding beauty to the garden while working as natural pest deterrents. Marigolds are especially good at keeping aphids and nematodes in check, and nasturtiums help with squash bugs and beetles, making them great garden teammates.

Foes: Winter squash doesn't do well in tight quarters with certain crops. **Potatoes** compete for space and nutrients underground, which can lead to stunted growth on both sides. **Tomatoes** share some of the same disease risks—like blights and fungal infections—so keeping them apart can help prevent problems from spreading. **Cucumbers** might seem like a natural pair, but they attract many of the same pests. Planting them together increases the chances of an infestation, especially from squash bugs and cucumber beetles. When planning your patch, keep winter squash with allies, and give it plenty of room to sprawl.

Leek

Onions

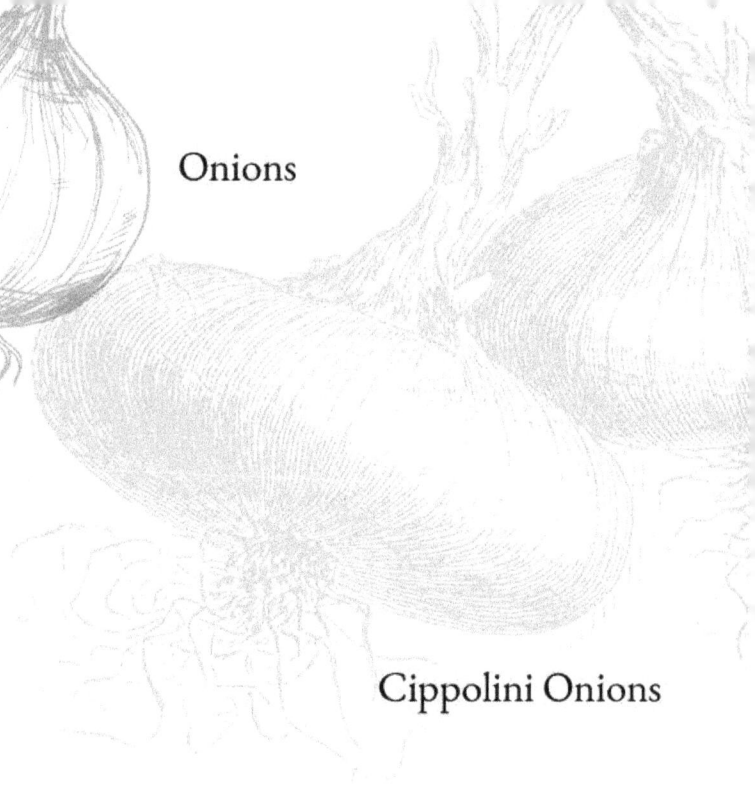

Cippolini Onions

Shallot

Amaryllidaceae

Amaryllidaceae Family

The Amaryllidaceae family includes a variety of fragrant, hardy, and versatile plants, many of which are staples in kitchens and gardens alike. From stunning flowers to flavorful bulbs, these plants offer both beauty and utility.

Garlic

Red onions

AMARYLLIDACEAE

Garden Gold

- **Garlic (Hardneck vs. Softneck):** *Flavorful bulbs-hardneck for robust taste and scapes, softneck for longer storage.*
- **Onions (Red, White, Yellow; Long Day vs. Short Day; Storage vs. Sweet):** *Versatile kitchen staples with types suited for every climate and use.*
- **Leeks:** *Mild, onion-like stalks, perfect for soups, stews, and roasting.*
- **Shallots:** *Sweet, delicate onions, ideal for gourmet cooking and dressings.*

AMARYLLIDACEAE FAMILY

This family includes onions, garlic, leeks, and chives—garden essentials known for their pungent aroma and pest-repelling superpowers. If there were a veggie that should wear a cape and be called the Protector of the Garden, it's these guys. Their strong scents work wonders in keeping pests at bay, which is why we love to border garden beds with these aromatic defenders. I have a confession. I don't grow green onions, scallions or any of the like. Here's why: the tops and thinning of onions, the tops of leeks and shallots keeps me full of the precious little greens, motivates me to keep up with the "pruning" and frees up space for other beauties in the garden. They really are an underrated star of the garden. Versatile in the kitchen, they add flavor to dishes from all cuisines. Plus, they're easy to grow—even for beginners!

Friends
Amaryllidaceae plants pair beautifully with almost any veggies, but especially well with carrots, tomatoes, and peppers. Their natural pest-repelling properties make them excellent companions for a healthy, thriving garden. I put them at the perimeter where they can do the most good.

Foes
The Allium family (onions, garlic, leeks, chives, etc.) has a strong scent and certain chemical compounds that can inhibit the growth of some plants. Three feet is usually plenty of space so I try to plant on opposite sides of the bed. If you notice issues, plant these farther away: beans, peas, carrots, beets, asparagus, and fennel.

Soil

Members of the Amaryllidaceae family thrive in rich, well-drained soil with a neutral to slightly acidic pH (6.0-7.0). Before planting, enrich the soil with compost or well-rotted manure to promote healthy growth. Proper drainage is key to avoiding bulb rot.

Fun Fact

Garlic and onions don't just spice up your meals—they're packed with allicin, a natural compound known for its antimicrobial properties. Think of them as garden superheroes with hidden powers!

Size

Amaryllidaceae plants are typically medium-sized. Onions and garlic form bulbs underground, while leeks and chives grow tall, slender foliage above ground. Their compact size makes them an adaptable choice for any garden layout.

Temperature and Light

These plants thrive in full sun but can tolerate partial shade. They prefer cooler growing conditions, with ideal temperatures ranging from 50°F to 75°F (10°C to 24°C). They're perfect for spring and fall planting seasons.

Watering

Consistent moisture is crucial, especially during early growth and bulb formation. Avoid overwatering, as soggy soil can lead to root and bulb rot. Water in the morning to allow foliage to dry out during the day, reducing the risk of fungal diseases. Mulching around the plants helps retain soil moisture and suppresses weeds.

Pests and Diseases

Amaryllidaceae plants are tough, but they aren't invincible. Here are some tips to tackle common issues:

- **Thrips:** Combat these tiny pests by spraying plants with a gentle stream of water to dislodge them. Just do this early in the day, when there is plenty of sunshine so you don't end up with fungal issues. You can use an organic neem oil for persistent infestations. Planting marigolds nearby can also help repel thrips naturally.

- **Fungal Diseases:** Prevent issues like downy mildew and white rot by improving airflow around plants. Space them adequately and avoid watering overhead. Morning watering ensures leaves dry quickly, further reducing fungal risks. Regularly remove dead or diseased foliage to maintain garden hygiene.

Onion

Difficulty Level: Moderate

Best For: Home cooks who love fresh, homegrown flavor.

Favorite Varieties:
- Dakota Tears: A flavorful, long-storing variety.
- Walla Walla: Sweet, mild, and perfect for fresh eating.
- Cabaret: A stunning county fair favorite for its unique shape and gorgeous color. This mild onion is sweet and excellent for eating fresh or cooked.

Growing Guide:
- Birthday: about 7-14 days from seed.
- Days to Maturity: 100-120 days.
- Ready to Thin for Green Onions: 30-50 days.
- When to Start: Start indoors 8-10 weeks before the last frost or plant sets outdoors in early spring.
- Special Spacing Requirements: 4-6 inches apart in rows 12-18 inches apart. You can pick up a pound of bulbs pretty economically, and that is usually more than enough for 4 raised beds.
- Light Requirements: Full sun.
- Special Care Notes:
  Onions are shallow-rooted and need consistent moisture. Mulching helps keep the soil cool and prevents weeds.

Harvesting:

- **How to Harvest:** Gently lift bulbs from the soil with a pitchfork or shovel fork. Give plenty of space to avoid damaging the bulb.
- **When to Harvest:** You can harvest for fresh use as soon as the bulb has formed. To store onions well, wait until the tops brown and fall over and begin to dry out. This allows the brown papery skin to thicken.
- **Storage Tips:** Cure in a warm, dry, well-ventilated area for 2-3 weeks, then store in a cool, dark place. After pulling from the ground, you'll want to trim the roots and cure them in a shady spot, safe from moisture (a garage works). Some people like to braid onions like garlic. Beware that the onion stems are not always strong enough to hold the larger onions. I recommend trimming one inch from the top and storing in a mesh bag or basket.

Pro Tips & Quirks

- **Start with bulbs or transplants** in your first year—onions are one of the easiest plants to grow! If you're feeling adventurous, check out Deep River Garden's website or Instagram for tips on starting from seed.
- **Trick:** When transplanting, trim the tops back to 6 inches to encourage better root growth.
- **Quirk:** Onions are day-length sensitive, so choose varieties suited to your region. It may seem counterintuitive, but cooler zones need long-day varieties due to the longer daylight hours in the summer.

LONG DAY VS. SHORT DAY ONIONS

Let me explain —

- Short-day onions (which need less sunlight) are best for southern regions because onions are planted in the fall, like garlic is in the north. Southern areas have shorter days during the winter and early spring, which is when the onions are growing.
- Long-day onions (which need more sunlight) are suited for northern regions where the growing season is through the summer and there are more hours of sunlight.

Friends: Onions are some of the easiest-going garden neighbors around. They do especially well alongside

lettuce, carrots, and even **strawberries.** Their strong scent helps confuse pests, which makes them a great companion for many crops. In fact, onions get along with just about everything—tucking them in around the perimeter is a smart move.

Foes: That said, onions aren't the best fit with **beans** and **peas.** Legumes can be a little sensitive to alliums. Planting them too close can slow down growth for both crops. No need for a major separation—just keep them on opposite sides of the bed and everyone will be fine.

Garlic

Difficulty Level: Easy

Best For: Gardeners who want a flavorful payoff for a fall planting.

While some would argue you can sow this in the spring and get a decent crop, I hold that it is not worth it. I am in Zone 5B/6A and here, this must be fall-sown for bulbs worth harvesting. Plan on planting in the fall.

Favorite Varieties
- **Music** (Hardneck): Spicy, robust flavor and easy to peel.
- **California Early** (Softneck): Mild flavor, stores well.

Growing Guide
- **Birthday:** when planted in the spring, sprouts will start to emerge very early spring.
- **Days to Maturity:** 8-9 months.
- **When to Start:** Plant individual cloves in fall, 4-6 weeks before the ground freezes.
- **Special Spacing Requirements:** 4-6 inches deep, 6 inches apart in rows 12 inches apart.
- **Light Requirements:** Full sun.

Special Care Notes
Mulch heavily after planting to protect bulbs over winter—think 4 inches of straw. In the spring, use liquid fertilizer weekly until leaves begin to yellow, about 2 weeks before harvest. OR side-dress with compost and

finish with a sprinkle of organic granular fertilizers designed for onions and garlic.

Harvesting

- **When to Harvest:** When the bottom 2-3 leaves are brown but the upper leaves are still green (Early July).
- **How to Harvest:** Loosen the soil gently with a fork before pulling.
- **Storage Tips:** Cure for 2-4 weeks in a dry, ventilated area, then store in a cool, dark spot.

Pro Tips & Quirks

- **Trick:** Use garlic scapes (flower stems) for an asparagus-like early harvest.
- **Quirk:** Each planted clove produces one whole bulb—talk about a return on investment!

Friends: Garlic pulls its weight in the garden—both in the kitchen and as a natural pest repellent. It gets along well with **tomatoes, peppers,** and **carrots,** all of which thrive in similar soil conditions. These buddies benefit from garlic's strong scent, which helps keep pests like aphids, spider mites, and root maggots at bay.

Foes: Garlic doesn't mix well with **asparagus or beans.** These crops compete for nutrients and space, and when planted together, neither tends to perform their best. Give garlic its own section or plant it near crops that appreciate its presence. Garlic does best when given its own space. It does not perform well when pushed on spacing.

Leeks

Difficulty Level: Moderate

Best For: Gourmet cooks and gardeners who love unique crops.

Leeks are amazing in soups. While many only eat the white end of the leek, the whole leek can be enjoyed and has an amazing mild flavor. Dehydrate the green tops to add to soups and stews for winter.

Favorite Variety

- **King Richard:** Early, tender, and mild.

Growing Guide

- Start from seedlings.
- **Days to Maturity** (LONG GROWER): 90-120 days and may sit in the garden until well after the last frost.
- **When to Start:** Start indoors 8-10 weeks before the last frost. Or plant transplants after the last frost. Leek transplants look fragile but they are surprisingly hardy. The little wisps of plants do grow.
- **Special Spacing Requirements**: 6 inches apart in rows 12 inches apart.
- **Light Requirements:** Full sun.

Special Care Notes

Sow Deep Hack: Use a large dibble or similar tool to make 4-inch-deep planting holes. Drop your leeks in and let them grow without backfilling the hole entirely. Over time, as you cultivate around the plants, the soil will naturally hill up around the stems, creating a beautifully blanched, tender white section—no extra hilling required! If you prefer the traditional method, mound soil around the base as the plant grows for the same effect.

Harvesting

- **When to Harvest:** When stems are 1 inch thick.
- **How to Harvest:** Pull gently or lift with a fork.
- **Storage Tips:** Store in the fridge for up to two weeks or freeze for long-term use.

Pro Tips & Quirks

- **Trick:** Trim roots and tops slightly when transplanting for sturdier growth.
- **Quirk:** Leeks are incredibly cold-tolerant and can overwinter in many climates. Counterintuitive, but give these guys a shock of cold and they will be sweeter for it.

Shallots

Difficulty Level: Moderate

Best For: Foodies who love their fancy French dishes.

Favorite Varieties

- **Cuisse de Poulet du Poitou:** Sweet, mild, and classic French shallots.
- **Matador:** Large, flavorful bulbs.

Growing Guide

- **Birthday:** about 8-10 days
- **Days to Maturity:** 90-120 days
- **When to Start:** Plant in early spring or fall, depending on your region. Sow bulbs in the fall for an early crop. If sown in the spring, be sure to grow from "spring sow" bulbs.
- **Special Spacing Requirements:** 6 inches apart in rows 12 inches apart.
- **Light Requirements:** Full sun.

Special Care Notes:

Keep soil consistently moist during bulb formation. Ease up on the water prior to harvest.

Harvesting

- **When to Harvest:** When tops dry out and fall over.
- **How to Harvest:** Dig gently with a fork to avoid damaging bulbs.
- **Storage Tips:** Cure in a warm, dry spot for 2-3 weeks before storing.

Pro Tips & Quirks

- **Save Money:** Save your best bulbs for replanting next season.
- **Trim the Tops!** If your spring is warmer than usual, you'll notice vigorous growth, so trim those tops. This not only gets you an additional crop but makes the bulbs grow bigger. Even if the spring is cool, by early summer, these guys will need a good haircut.
- **Quirk:** Shallots grow in clusters—each planted bulb yields several new ones. This surprised me my first time when I saw this flattened cluster of shallot cloves. I was ecstatic!

Friends: Shallots get along wonderfully with carrots, lettuce, and tomatoes. These companions not only help deter pests but also thrive in similar soil conditions, making them great neighbors for shallots. Their presence can keep pests like aphids and root maggots at bay, ensuring a healthier harvest for everyone.

Foes: On the flip side, beans and peas aren't the best match for shallots. Both compete for nutrients and space, which can stunt the growth of both crops. It's best to plant shallots on the opposite side of the bed from these legumes to keep things growing strong.

Part 3

Calendars and Schedules

From Planning to Planting: Bringing Your Garden to Life

Now that we've covered the key players in your garden—veggies, flowers, and everything in between—it's time to put that knowledge into action. This section is all about the how to of implementation: getting your hands in the dirt and making a plan that works for you. This section is all about making your garden work for you, no matter your space, time, or experience level. Ready to dive in? Let's get growing!

ZERO-TO-SIXTY PREP SEASON CHART
This 36-day checklist will take you from a bare patch of land to a fully prepped, ready-to-grow space.

SUCCESSION PLANTING & OVERWINTERING
Once you've had a successful season, it's time to level up.

MONTHLY PLANTING CALENDAR
(With Space for Notes!)

GARDEN PLANS
9Big to Beginner Sized)

36-DAY ZERO-TO-SIXTY GET GROWING GUIDE

Welcome to the 36-Day Zero-to-Sixty Get Growing Guide!

You may have purchased this detailed guide to kick-start your garden journey checklist. I am including it in the book as a bonus! This is a step-by-step resource to help you get growing fast. I designed it to take you from zero to fully prepped and ready to plant in just 36 days with simple, 15-minute tasks that will keep you moving forward without overwhelm.

While I recommend starting this process in the fall, giving your soil time to settle and your mind time to ease into the season, you can absolutely start as late as April and still be ready to grow by May in Zones 5-6. The earlier you start, the more wiggle room you'll have to miss a day or adjust for unexpected hiccups (because let's be honest, life happens).

The beauty of this plan is momentum. Small, consistent steps build a solid foundation for a thriving garden. No single task will take more than 15 minutes. By the time you reach the end, you'll have everything in place—your garden layout, soil, seeds, tools, and a game plan for success.

How to Use This Guide

- Each day, spend just 15 minutes on the designated task. That's it. No stress, no marathon workdays.
- If you're starting late, no worries—just pick up where you are and adjust as needed.
- Some days are dedicated to reading this book (yes, really!). Consider it part of your training— gardening is as much about knowledge as it is about action.
- If you miss a day, don't sweat it. Just keep going. Progress is the goal, not perfection.

Are you ready? Take a deep breath—Let's get growing!

WEEK 1 SET THE STAGE

Quick Start
36 days, 15 Minutes a day

Week 1: Laying the Foundation
This week, we're going to focus on learning and laying the groundwork for your garden. Just 15 minutes a day, and we're off to a calm, smooth start.

Day 1 Read this book! Yes, I mean it— just 15 minutes of reading to start your garden journey.

Day 2 Create your garden space plan: Mark out the garden space with twine and stakes.

Day 3 Check your space. Take a quick look at your garden area. Work on your sunmap. Are there any obstacles, like a fence or a tree that might get in the way? Make sure your spot gets 8-12 hours of sun!

Day 4 Read this book! —grab a warm beverage and relax while reading.

Look for lush grass, full sun

Avoid shade spots, puddles of water or dry dead grass

Budget Talks

Day 5 Decide on Budget: Use the information in chapter 2 to decide on the size and cost of your garden.

Day 6 Review your seed list. Take a look at your garden plan and make sure your seed choices match your layout. If you have the 15 Minute Gardener Handbook make sure to complete the *Veggies We Eat* Chart and Companion planting guide. Swap out any veggie you do not want.

Day 7: Rest and Read *15 Minute Gardener* or browse your favorite seed catalog.

Gather Supplies and Set Up Your Garden

Day 8 Create your composting system: You don't have to go all out—just gather some basics like a worm bin or compost pile location.

Day 9 Research soil quality: Spend a few minutes reading up on soil types (loamy, clay, sandy). Don't worry about becoming an expert, just a quick check to know what kind of soil you'll need. And decide if you are going to purchase or use local free sources for soil.

Day 10 Rest day. Read or listen to gardening podcast.

Day 11 Finalize composting options. If you're not sure about composting, look into buying compost from a local garden center. It's a simple alternative.

Day 12 Order soil or compost. The rule of thumb is 1 yard per 4x8x2ft bed. Soil settles so I like to get 25% extra. Look into your town's compost program. Many towns have excellent leaf mulch and wood chips available to residents for free or low cost.

Day 13 Gather your tools. Check that you have all the basics: trowel, watering can, gloves, spade (pointed shovel), clippers. If not, order what you're missing.

Day 14: Rest. Order *15 Minute Gardener: You Can Grow* to get detailed planting plans, full-year calendars, bullet proof planting methods, budget breaks downs and an invaluable plant-by-plant companion planting guide and care cheat sheet. Ask me questions on social media - I want to help where I can.

A little prep now will make planting a breeze!

Day 15:
- Set up your garden layout. Put together Raised Bed 1

Day 16:
- Set up your garden layout. Put together Raised Bed 2

Day 17:
- Set up your garden layout. Put together Raised Bed 3

Day 18:
- Set up your garden layout. Put together Raised Bed 4

Day 19 & 20
- Fill Raised beds–Follow the Layering Technique in Chapter____

Day 21:
- Rest Day–You're getting really close to the end. Slip some reading time in. Keep going!

Raised Bed Sources--

- Check out our amazon store for some of our favorite budget friendly varieties.
- If you have the cash, invest in quality because a raised bed should last years.
- DIY: Anna White has great plans. Remember that my recommendation is 18 inches minimum, 2ft is ideal. You need that space for root growth and vibrant plant production.

You're in the final stretch now!

This week, we're prepping for actual planting.

Day 22:

Gather your fertilizer. You will not need it right away but it is good to have it on hand.

Day 23:

Review your seed-starting and transplant list. Find a trusted local nursery or grower at your local farm market to buy seedlings. Avoid the big box stores unless they are the only option.

Day 24:

Make seed plan or chose one of the plans in this book.

Day 25:

Prepare your watering system. Make sure your watering cans are clean and your hoses are ready to go. It's a small task, but it'll save you time later.

Day 26:

Double-check your garden plan. Have a quick glance over your garden layout. Make sure everything feels aligned and personalization for your tastes has been made. Double-check that you have the right space for each plant.

Day 27:

Order any last-minute supplies. Use Chip Drop to get free mulch for your Garden or order natural mulch for around your garden beds to make the whole space feel finished and keep weeds down.

Day 28:

Rest. Celebrate. You have come so far.

WEEK 5: FINAL TOUCHES

You're almost there!

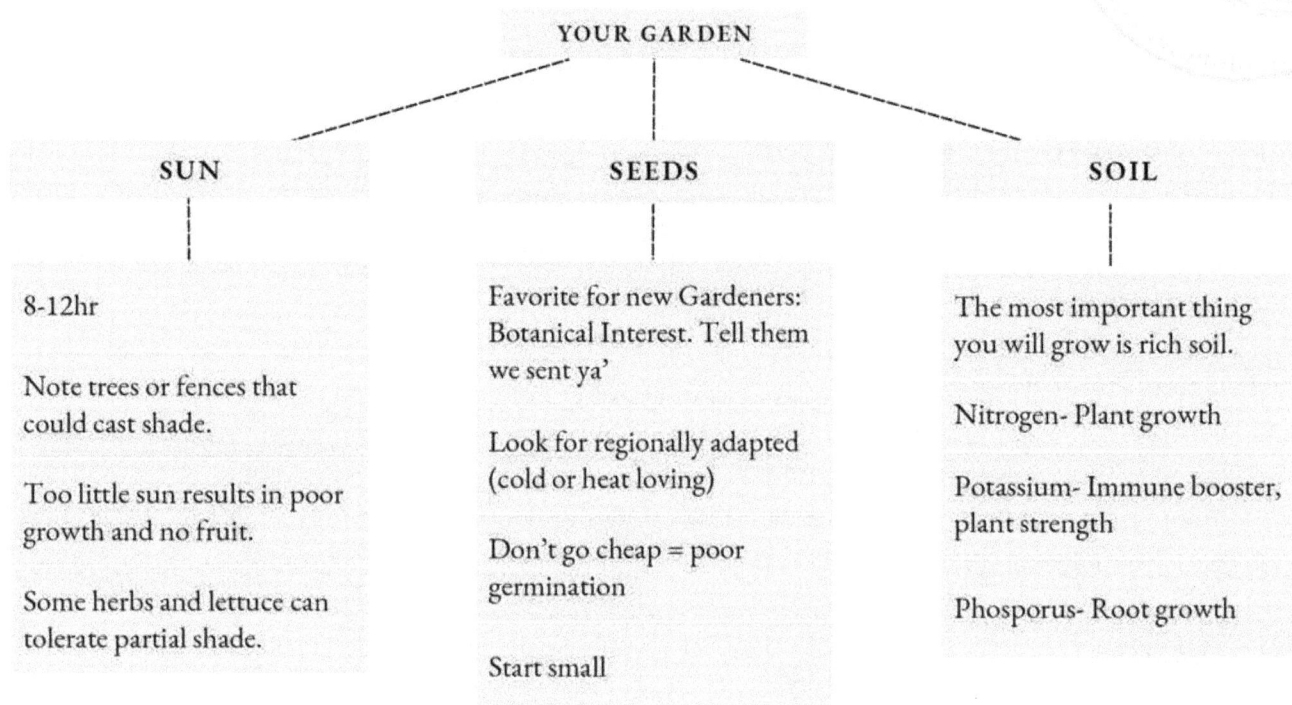

```
                          YOUR GARDEN


       SUN                  SEEDS                  SOIL


  8-12hr              Favorite for new Gardeners:   The most important thing
                      Botanical Interest. Tell them  you will grow is rich soil.
  Note trees or fences that  we sent ya'
  could cast shade.                                 Nitrogen- Plant growth
                      Look for regionally adapted
  Too little sun results in poor  (cold or heat loving)   Potassium- Immune booster,
  growth and no fruit.                              plant strength
                      Don't go cheap = poor
  Some herbs and lettuce can  germination           Phosporus- Root growth
  tolerate partial shade.
                      Start small
```

Day 29:

Prepare your seed packets. Label your seed packets and organize them. You're going to feel so accomplished when it's all sorted. Use the Recipe box method. Get a recipe box from the dollar store. Sort seeds one of two ways- Alphabetically OR if you are succession planting savvy, sort seeds by the month you will start or direct sow.

Day 30:

Review your compost system. Check on those worms if you decided to learn that skill. Either way make sure your system is ready for use when the season picks up.

Day 31 Catch Up Day: Life happens. Look over the steps. What did you miss or what do you need more time to digest?

WEEK 5: FINAL TOUCHES

Day 32:

Mulch: Check tools and seedlings. Use cardboard and mulch to mulch around your garden.

Day 33:

Prepare for your first planting day. Purchase starts around May 15th. Look over the Garden plan and note any tweaks. Onions, spring shallots, radishes and Kale can be sown.

Day 34:

Gather any extra supplies. If you've forgotten anything, now's the time to grab it. A quick check to make sure you've got everything.

Day 35:

Tell your friends about this resource. People who garden with friends grow better.

Day 36: Finish the Book. Share a photo! Connect with us on Facebook @DeepRiverGardens or Instagram @15MinGardener

Monthly Planting Calendar

How to Use this Calendar

1. Date your notes: Each time you complete a task, jot down the date it was done. This helps you keep track of timing and conditions for future years. You don't need long notes.

2. Bookmark this page: Save the checklist as a go-to resource for each month. Reviewing it at the start of every month helps you stay on top of tasks without forgetting anything.

3. Add personal notes: As you go along, feel free to jot down observations about what worked well or any changes to the plan (weather conditions, pest outbreaks, etc.).

With this structure, you'll build a solid gardening journal for each year. The more notes you take, the better your garden planning will be for future seasons. Pro tip—date your entries. As the years pass, you will 100% wonder what year you wrote that note.

NOTE: I live in Upstate New York near Lake Ontario. This makes our winters slower to start but harsher and prone to heavy snows after January. Knowing your first and last frost dates will be the most powerful guide to determining the best date to put your plants into the ground. You can adjust this schedule to your start date by counting backward from your last frost date the number of weeks it takes for your transplant to mature. That means if my tomatoes take 8 weeks to reach transplant size, I want to start my tomato seeds in mid-March. With the internet, we can see what the whole world is doing, but we need to know *our* climate so we can grow in sync with it.

January

Seeds to Start	Tasks
	Maintain Monday: Order seeds; gather supplies for seed starting.
	Trim Tuesday: Determine budget, garden size, and crops.
	Weed Wednesday: Check on saved seeds/tubers. Review last year's crops. Weed out poor-performing crops.
	Pest-Free Thursday: Inspect seed storage, containers for bugs, clean, and store.
	Harvest Friday: Try a new recipe with a food you hope to grow or grew last year.
	Prune & Plant Saturday: Start herbs inside on window ledge. Narrow seed catalogs to 2-3 favorite options. Finish seed order.
	Review & Rest Sunday: Read notes on past garden. Research an issue and ask a question @deepriverfamilyfarm Instagram.

February

Seeds to Start	Tasks
(Broccoli, Cabbage, Tomatoes, Peppers 8-12 Weeks before last frost. Some flowers should be started now, check package.)	Maintain Monday: Order seeds; gather supplies for seed starting.
	Trim Tuesday: Determine budget, garden size, and crops.
	Weed Wednesday: Check on saved seeds/tubers. Review last year's crops. Weed out poor-performing crops.
	Pest-Free Thursday: Inspect seed storage, containers for bugs, clean, and store.
	Harvest Friday: Try a new recipe with a food you hope to grow or grew last year.
	Prune & Plant Saturday: Start herbs inside on window ledge. Narrow seed catalogs to 2-3 favorite options. Finish seed order.
	Review & Rest Sunday: Read notes on past garden. Research an issue and ask a question @deepriverfamilyfarm Instagram.

March

Seeds to Start	Tasks
Onions, Peas, Kale, Herbs, Winter greens 8 weeks before last frost	Maintain Monday: Prep garden beds, amend soil.
	Trim Tuesday: Prune & Plan, ensure seeds are ordered and garden plans solidified.
	Weed Wednesday: Prep garden tools.
	Pest-Free Thursday: Check seedlings for damping off/mold.
	Harvest Friday: Enjoy fresh herbs. Trim onion seedlings if sown.
	Prune & Plant Saturday: Direct sow peas, radishes when soil is workable (end of March), cover at night.
	Review & Rest Sunday.

April

Seeds to Start	Tasks
Flowers (Marigold, Zinnia, Sunflower), Lettuce, Spinach, Swiss Chard, Beets.	Maintain Monday: Order seeds; gather supplies for seed starting.
	Trim Tuesday: Determine budget, garden size, and crops.
	Weed Wednesday: Check on saved seeds/tubers. Review last year's crops. Weed out poor-performing crops.
	Pest-Free Thursday: Inspect seed storage, containers for bugs, clean, and store.
	Harvest Friday: Try a new recipe with a food you hope to grow or grew last year.
	Prune & Plant Saturday: Start herbs inside on window ledge. Narrow seed catalogs to 2-3 favorite options. Finish seed order.
	Review & Rest Sunday: Read notes on past garden. Research an issue and ask a question @deepriverfamilyfarm Instagram.

May

Seeds to Start	Tasks
Transplant/Sow after danger of frost has passed: Tomatoes, Peppers, Cucumbers, Beans, Carrots, Beets	After last frost (mid-May), plant tomatoes, peppers, cucumbers. Direct sow beans, carrots, beets.
	Maintain Monday: Ensure consistent watering.
	Trim Tuesday: Check for proper spacing between seedlings.
	Weed Wednesday: Remove weeds competing with young seedlings.
	Pesty Thursday: Monitor for pests like cutworms and aphids.
	Harvest Friday: Start picking early greens.
	Prune & Plant Saturday: Finish transplanting or prune tomatoes and peppers.

June

Seeds to Start	Tasks
Keep sowing veggies. Switch to warm season lettuce to prevent bitter leaves.	Maintain Monday: Water deeply.
	Trim Tuesday: Prune tomato plants and remove suckers.
	Weed Wednesday: Continue mulching to suppress weeds.
	Pesty Thursday: Watch for cabbage worms; handpick if necessary.
	Harvest Friday: Pick spinach and early peas.
	Prune & Plant Saturday: Fertilize heavy feeders like squash and tomatoes.
	Review & Rest Sunday.

July

Seeds to Start	Tasks
Kale, Broccoli, Cabbage, Radishes, Lettuce, Fall Peas	Maintain Monday: Harvest midseason crops and water deeply.
	Trim Tuesday: Trim heavy foliage for better airflow.
	Weed Wednesday: Keep removing weeds competing for nutrients.
	Pesty Thursday: Treat pest outbreaks with organic methods.
	Harvest Friday: Continue enjoying tomatoes, cucumbers, and other summer crops.
	Prune & Plant Saturday: Succession sow fall crops like kale and broccoli.
	Review & Rest Sunday.

August

Seeds to Start	Tasks
Bush beans, dwarf peas, Lettuce, If your last frost date is mid Octorber you have 75 days to work with. Make sure to plan accordingly	Maintain Monday: Harvest midseason crops and water deeply.
	Trim Tuesday: Trim heavy foliage for better airflow.
	Weed Wednesday: Keep removing weeds competing for nutrients.
	Pesty Thursday: Treat pest outbreaks with organic methods.
	Harvest Friday: Continue enjoying tomatoes, cucumbers, and other summer crops.
	Prune & Plant Saturday: Succession sow fall crops like kale and broccoli.
	Review & Rest Sunday.

September

Seeds to Start	Tasks
Kale, Broccoli, Cabbage, Radishes, Lettuce	Maintain Monday: Harvest midseason crops and water deeply.
	Trim Tuesday: Trim heavy foliage for better airflow.
	Weed Wednesday: Keep removing weeds. Stay on top of bug checks.
	Pesty Thursday: Treat pest outbreaks with organic methods.
	Harvest Friday: Continue enjoying tomatoes, cucumbers, and other summer crops.
	Prune & Plant Saturday: Succession sow fall crops like kale and broccoli.
	Review & Rest Sunday.

October

Seeds to Start	Tasks
Tomatoes, Peppers, Squash, Beans, Kale, Spinach	Maintain Monday: Water consistently and deeply.
	Trim Tuesday: Prune overgrown vines and remove dead leaves.
	Weed Wednesday: Keep beds clean for fall sowing.
	Pesty Thursday: Monitor for spider mites and aphids.
	Harvest Friday: Preserve or store excess harvests.
	Prune & Plant Saturday: Start sowing spinach and kale for fall.
	Review & Rest Sunday.

November

Seeds to Start	Tasks
Cover Crop	Maintain Monday: Add compost and mulch to protect soil.
	Trim Tuesday: Finalize notes on this year's garden.
	Weed Wednesday: Remove debris and prep for cover crops.
	Pesty Thursday: Protect overwintering greens from frost with covers.
	Harvest Friday: Gather the last of kale and parsley.
	Prune & Plant Saturday: Sow cover crops like clover or rye.
	Review & Rest Sunday: Reflect on successes and challenges.

December

Seeds to Start	Tasks
Tomatoes, Peppers, Squash, Beans, Kale, Spinach	Maintain Monday: Order seeds and inventory tools.
	Trim Tuesday: Review and dream of next season.
	Weed Wednesday: Clean tools and storage areas.
	Pesty Thursday: Inspect and repair garden equipment.
	Harvest Friday: Enjoy stored vegetables and winter squash. Dream of spring while sipping cocoa.

Deep River Girls' Tea:

Think of someone you could bless with a little **"Garden in a Basket"**:
A packet of heirloom seeds
A trusty hand trowel or mini pruners
A pair of garden gloves.
A notebook for dreaming and planning
A pottery mug for those early morning garden brainstorms.

Tuck it all in a basket, tie it with a ribbon.
Now you've planted friendship.

Planning for Next Year

As we look ahead to future growing seasons, we can think about ways to grow more in a small space. One way is to stagger your plantings and maximize your season yields by leaning into your different growing seasons. You can divide the year into three categories (four if you include the winter season):

Early Season

- Cool-Weather Crops: Start with lettuce, spinach, and peas. These thrive in the cooler temperatures of early spring and can be planted as soon as the soil is workable.

Midseason

- Heat-Loving Vegetables: Transition to tomatoes, peppers, and beans as the days grow warmer. These plants relish the heat and will reward you with bountiful harvests through the summer.

Late Season

- Fall Favorites: As the heat wanes, reclaim garden space for kale, carrots, and garlic. These crops thrive in cooler temperatures and can often withstand the first frosts.

Key Tools for Succession Success

Succession planting is something that takes some skill and finesse. Don't feel like you have to aim for all three seasons by year two or even three. Find the rhythm that works and is low pressure. Here's what you need to get started:

- **Garden Journal:** Track planting dates, harvests, and notes on what worked well. The more notes you take the more you will be able to refine your growing skills. My notes are messy and tattered but I have them and it is a treasure.
- **Calendar** (digital or paper) for monitoring. Use weather app to keep an eye on frost dates that can vary year to year. Mark expected germination and note when fertilization and harvest dates.
- **Seed Packets:** Pay attention to maturity dates to plan your planting transitions.

Succession Planting Schedule

You Can Grow MORE

Crop	Planting Intervals	Variety	Details
Arugula	Every 2 weeks	Rocket, Astro	Perfect for quick-growing salad greens; thrives in cooler weather.
Asian Greens	Every 2 weeks March-May / Sept	Minzuna, Celtuce	Perfect for quick-growing salad greens; thrives in cooler weather. Mild, peppery, antioxidant spinach flavor. Great for stir-fry and soups.
Basil	Every 2-3 weeks	Genovese, Thai	Stagger plantings to maintain a fresh supply for culinary use.
Basil (Medicinal)	Every 2-3 weeks	Tulsi, Lemon	Great for teas, pestos, and more. Pro tip: grow multiple varieties.
Beans	Every 2-3 weeks	Beans	Sow in intervals to keep the harvest coming all season.
Broccoli, Kale	Every 4 weeks	Broccoli, Kale	Plant for fall crops—perfect for cooler weather.
Carrots, Beets	Every 2-3 weeks	Carrots, Beets	Rotate planting for an endless supply of root veggies.
Cilantro	Every 2-3 weeks	Santo, Leisure	Direct sow regularly for fresh leaves; bolts quickly in summer heat.
Corn	Every 3 weeks	Silver Queen, Peaches & Cream	For a continuous, fresh sweet corn supply, sow in large batches frequently. Corn requires large, close plantings to pollinate well. Not great for small gardens.

Crop	Planting Intervals	Variety	Details
Cucumbers	Every 3-4 weeks	Marketmore, Boston Pickling	Plant successively for extended fresh harvests and pickling supplies.
Dill	Every 2-3 weeks	Bouquet, Fernleaf	Regular sowing ensures a steady supply for pickling or garnishing.
Mustard Greens	Every 2-3 weeks	Red Giant, Mizuna	Quick to mature, adds a peppery flavor to salads and dishes.
Pak Choi	Every 3 weeks	Baby Pak Choi, Joi Choi	Great for stir-fry; grows quickly and loves cooler temperatures.
Parsnips	Every 4-6 weeks	Hollow Crown, Gladiator	Best for cooler weather; stagger plantings for fall and early winter harvest.
Radishes	Every 2-3 weeks	Radishes	Radishes grow fast—direct sow for consistent harvests.
Scallions	Every 3 weeks	Evergreen Hardy White	Succession planting ensures a constant supply of fresh green onions.
Spinach, Lettuce	Every 2-3 weeks	Spinach, Lettuce	Sow seeds regularly for a continuous supply of fresh greens.
Swiss Chard	Every 3-4 weeks	Rainbow, Fordhook Giant	Harvest outer leaves while letting the plant continue to grow.
Turnips	Every 3-4 weeks	Purple Top, Tokyo Cross	Sow for tender roots and greens; ideal for fall harvests.
Zucchini	Every 4-6 weeks	Black Beauty, Cocozelle	Stagger plantings to extend harvest while avoiding overwhelm and to have back-up plantings when bug pressure becomes intense.

GROWING THROUGH THE SEASONS

Garden Plans for Every Space

We have **detailed garden plans** for many different garden sizes. One of the things I wanted most when just starting out was a plan that told me EXACTLY what to plant. Here you go. Remember, to customize, you can swap out members of the same family in the plans rather seamlessly as long as they don't have vastly different space requirements. For example, you could safely swap any variety of lettuce or broccoli with kale. This is where the FRIEND, FAMILY, FOE trifecta shines. There are LIMITLESS possibilities, and now you have years of easily adjustable garden beds.

Beginner-Sized Options:

Four 4x8 raised beds, including:
- **Lettuce Garden**—a continuous supply of lettuce and salad staples.
- **Canner's Garden**—so you can grow and preserve the flavors of the season.
- **Spring Garden**—A well-rounded variety of classic veggies.
- **Fall Garden**—Perfect succession for the fall garden.

With these tools, you'll be set up for success from **spring through fall**. Gardens come in all shapes and sizes. There's no one-size-fits-all approach. Need more growing space? Rather than add on endless boxes, I recommend another option.

On a final note: A BIG thank you to Keira and Sadie, who painstakingly drew these plans by hand.

CANNER'S GARDEN

Box 1 Planting Instructions:

Lettuce Head- 1-2 seeds every 6in (head)

OR

Scatter Sow (just sprinkle seed) evenly. Cut as loose leaf mix (you can get 2-3 cuttings)

Peppers- sow every 6-8in

Basil- Transplant 4 plants

Tomatoes- Transplant 4 plants

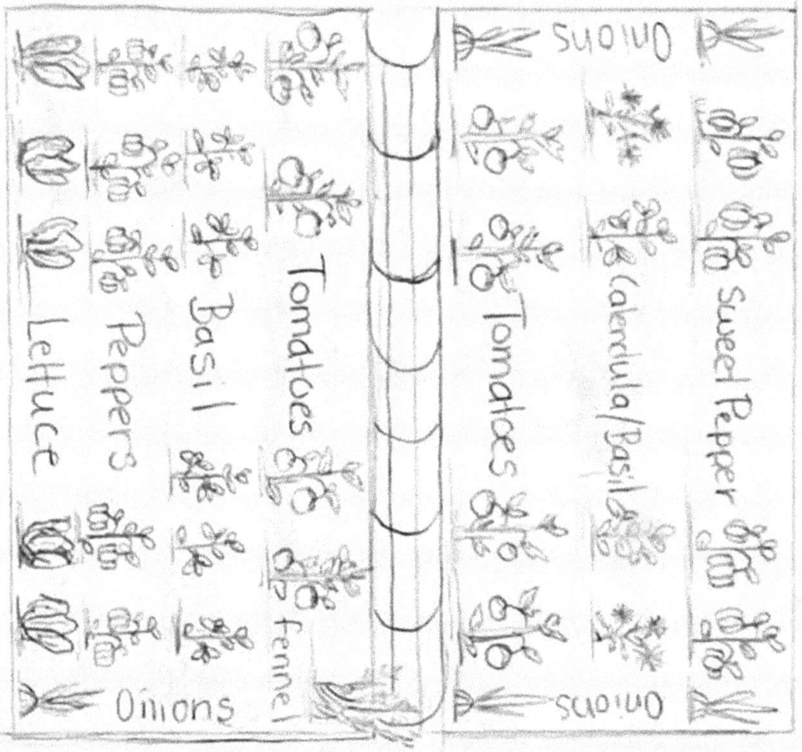

Box 3 Planting Instructions:

Tomatoes—4 plants every 12 in, Plant cherry tomatoes here.

Onions— Transplant every 4in on one side of box. (Shallots may also be substituted)

Calendula and Basil—(any herb/flower, Zinnia and Parsely etc.) Alternate plants every 6 in.

Peppers— sow every 6-8in

Box 2 Planting Instructions:

Bush Beans—1-2 seeds every 6in

OR

Carrots—Mix seeds with half sand and sprinkle two rows 12 in apart.

Cucumber— sow every 12 in

Onions— Transplant every 4in on one side of box

Dill—Sprinkle seed or transplant 2 plants.

Box 4 Planting Instructions:

Box 4 Planting Instructions:

Cucumber— sow every 12 in

Carrots—Mix seeds with half sand and sprinkle two rows 12 in apart.

Onions—Transplant every 4in on one side of box. (Shallots may also be substituted)

Onions—Transplant every 4in. On long side of box. (Shallots may also be substituted)

Herb of Choice- (Dill, Basil, Parsely) and/or Flower- Marigold/Zinnia

SALAD GARDEN

Box 1 Planting Instructions:

Radish- Scatter sow

Carrots— Mix seeds with half sand and sprinkle two rows 12 in apart.

Tomatoes— 4 plants every 12 in, Plant cherry tomatoes here.

Onions— Transplant every 4in on short sides of box. (Shallots may also be substituted)

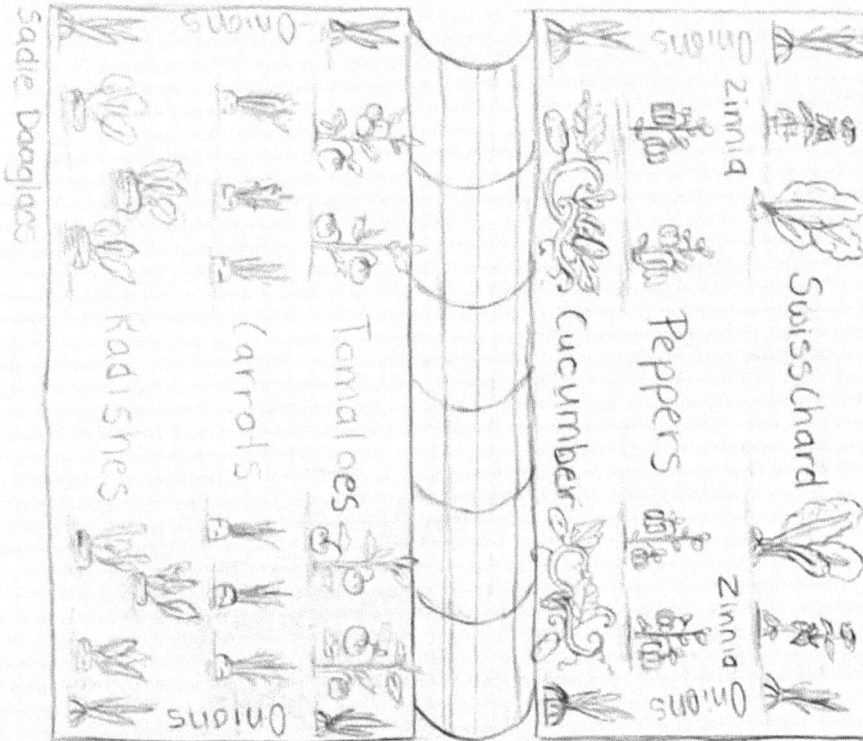

Box 2 Planting Instructions:

Swiss Chard- Scatter sow/ thin to 1 plant every 6 in. Use thinnings for salad.

Peppers— sow every 6-8in

Cucumber— sow every 12 in

Onions— Transplant every 4in on short sides of box.

Box 3 Planting Instructions:

Swiss Chard- Scatter sow/ thin to 1 plant every 6 in. Use thinnings for salad.

Sweet peas— sow 2-3 seeds every 4-6 in

Spinach— sow every 4 in

Beets— sow every 4in.

Onions— Transplant every 4in on short sides of box. (Shallots may also be substituted)

Box 4 Planting Instructions:

Herb/Flower- of choice Transplant every 6in.

Kale— Scatter sow. Thin to 1 plant every 6in

Tomatoes— 4 plants every 12 in, Plant cherry tomatoes here.

Onions— Transplant every 4in on short sides of box. (Shallots may also be substituted)

SPRING GARDEN

Box 1 Planting Instructions:

Radish- Scatter sow

Carrots—Mix seeds with half sand and sprinkle two rows 12 in apart.

Tomatoes—4 plants every 12 in, Plant cherry tomatoes here.

Onions—Transplant every 4in on short sides of box. (Shallots may also be substituted)

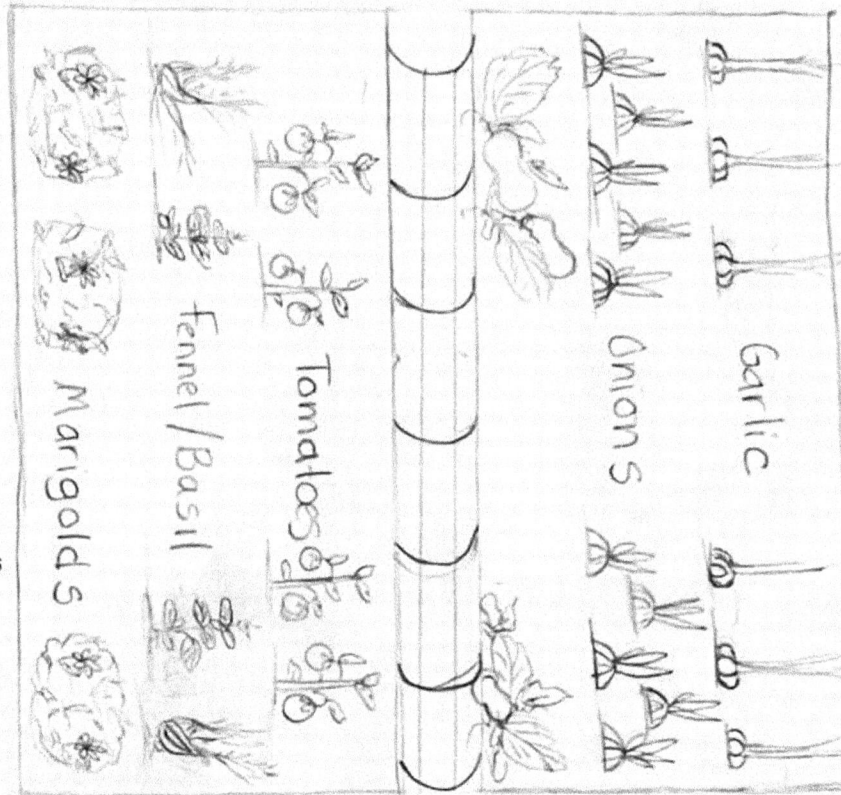

Marigolds

Fennel/Basil

Tomatoes

Box 2 Planting Instructions:

Garlic

Onions

Garlic—Sow every 6 in in fall-two rows

Onions—Transplant every 4in two rows

Melon of choice— sow 2 seeds every 12in. train to trellis. or transplant

Box 3 Planting Instructions:

Lettuce: Scatter sow/ thin to 1 plant every 6 in. Use thinnings for salad.

Beets— sow every 4 in

Beans—sow every 4in along trelis.

Optional—Plant herb/flower in corners

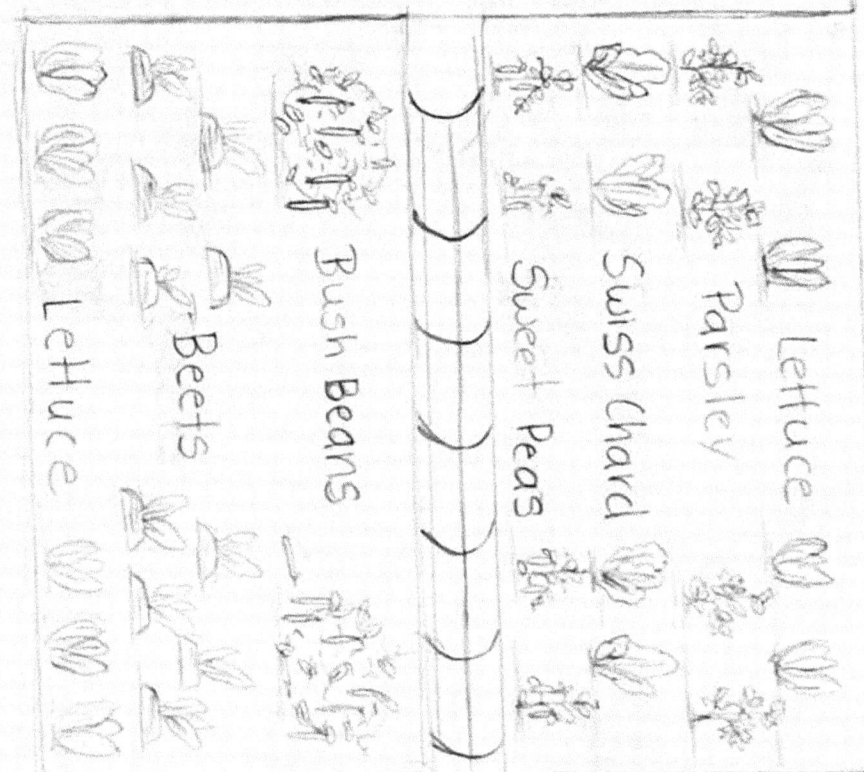

Lettuce

Beets

Bush Beans

Box 4 Planting Instructions:

Sweet Peas

Swiss Chard

Parsley

Lettuce

Lettuce Head- 1-2 seeds every 6in (head) **OR** **Scatter Sow** (just sprinkle seed) evenly. Cut as loose leaf mix (you can get 2-3 cuttings)

Herb/Flower- of **choice** Transplant every 6in.

Swiss Chard- Scatter sow/ thin to 1 plant every 6 in. Use thinnings for salad.

Sweet peas—sow2-3 seeds every 4-6 in.

FALL GARDEN

As spring crops are harvested, plant July/August for fall harvest. .

Box 1 Planting Instructions:

Herb/Flower—of choice Transplant every 6in.

Basil— Transplant 4 plants

Tomatoes— Transplant 4 plants- make sure this is an established transplant with a short harvest window

Box 2 Planting Instructions:

Herb/Flower- of choice Transplant every 6in.

Beets— sow every 4 in

(*Optional*) **Onions**— Transplant every 4in two rows

Winter Squash of choice— sow 2 seeds every 12in. train to trellis. If mellon plant stops producing late July remove and follow with fall peas OR WINTER Squash

Box 3 Planting Instructions:

Watermellon Radish/Radish-Scatter Sow (just sprinkle seed) evenly.

Spinach- Scatter sow/ thin to 1 plant every 6 in. Use thinnings for salad.

Sweet peas— sow2-3 seeds every 4-6 in.

Box 4 Planting Instructions:

Herb/Flower- of choice Transplant every 6in.

Swiss Chard- Scatter sow/ thin to 1 plant every 6 in. Use thinnings for salad.

Kale—Scatter sow. Thin to 1 plant every 6in

Winter Squash of choice— sow 2 seeds every 12in. train to trellis.

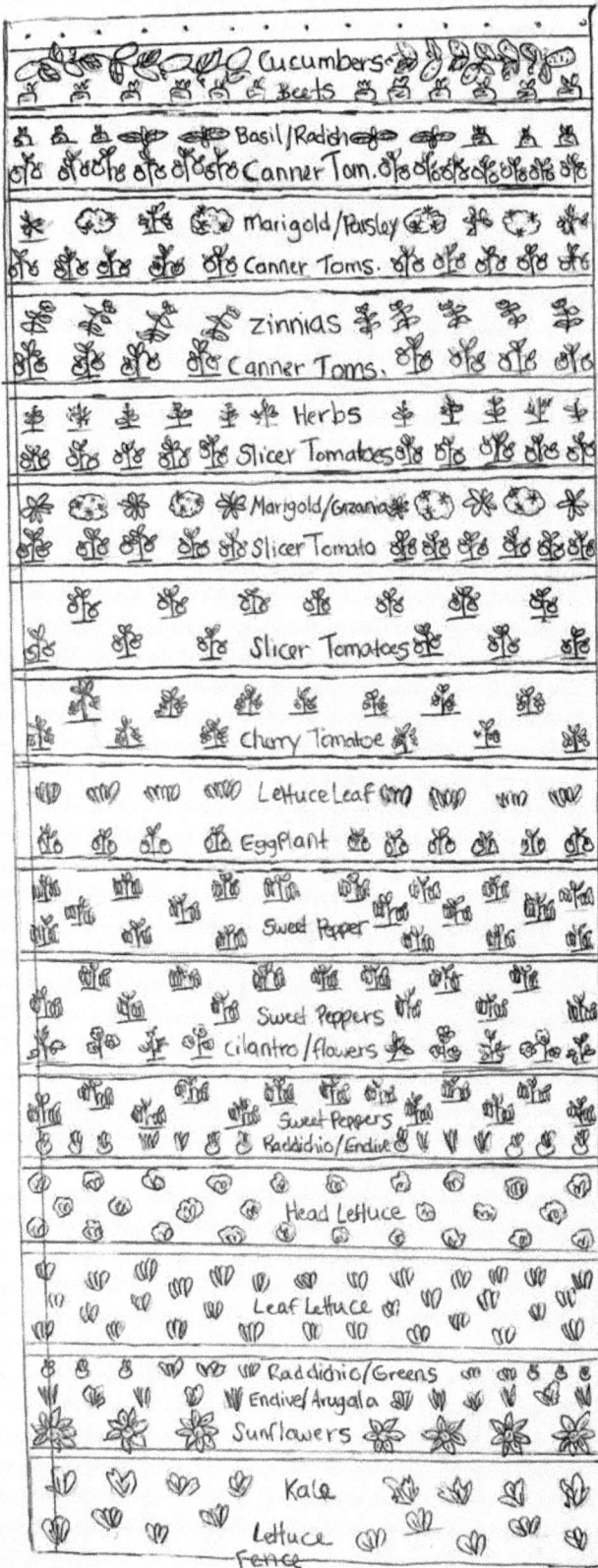

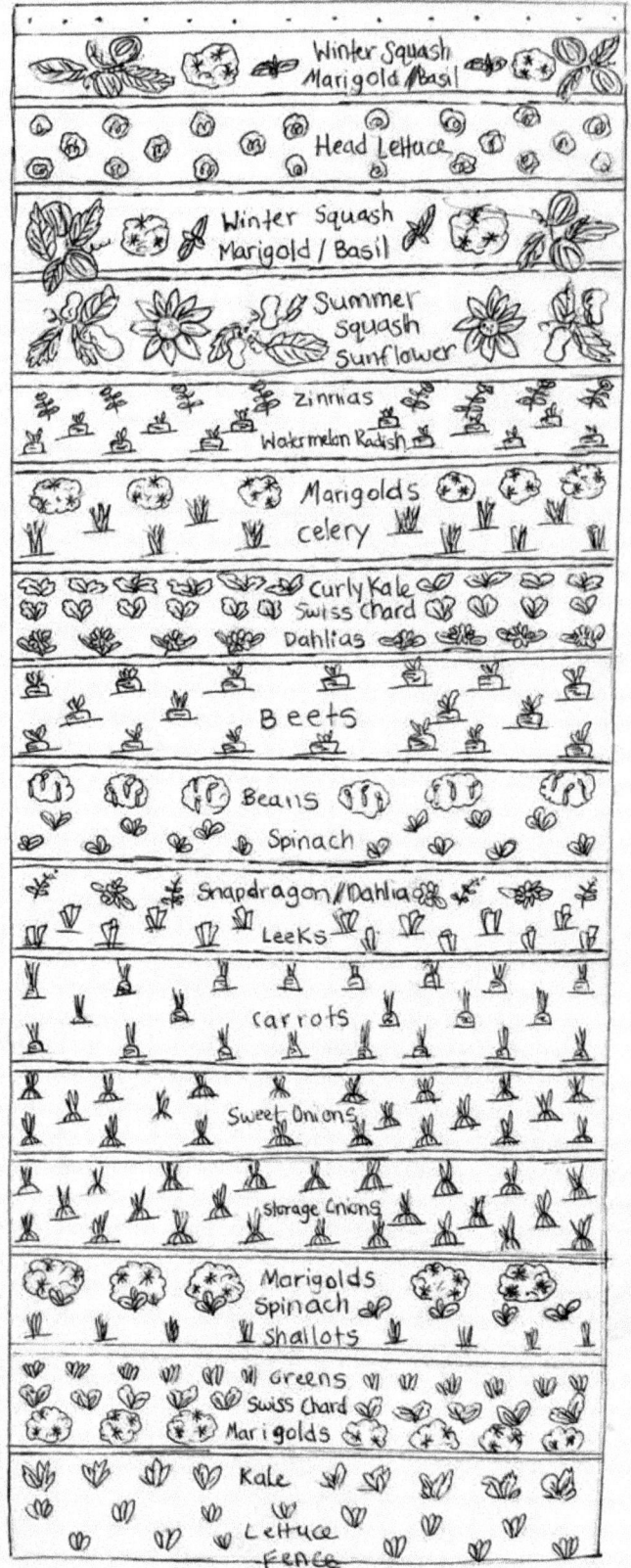

VICTORY GARDEN 1500 SQ FT

Bed A

10 x 64:

Cucumbers
Beets

Basil / Radish
Canner Tom.

Marigold / Parsley
Canner Toms.

Zinnias
Canner Toms.

Herbs
Slicer Tomatoes

Marigold / Grzania
Slicer Tomato

Slicer Tomatoes

Cherry Tomatoe

Lettuce Leaf
Eggplant

Sweet Pepper

Sweet Peppers
Cilantro / flowers

Sweet Peppers
Raddichio / Endive

Head Lettuce

Leaf Lettuce

Raddichio / Greens
Endive / Arugala
Sunflowers

Kale
Lettuce
Fence

Bed B

10 x 64:

Winter Squash
Marigold / Basil

Head Lettuce

Winter Squash
Marigold / Basil

Summer
Squash
Sunflower

Zinnias
Watermelon Radish

Marigolds
Celery

Curly Kale
Swiss Chard
Dahlias

Beets

Beans
Spinach

Snapdragon / Dahlia
Leeks

Carrots

Sweet Onions

Storage Onions

Marigolds
Spinach
Shallots

Greens
Swiss Chard
Marigolds

Kale
Lettuce
Fence

220

VICTORY GARDEN 1500 SQ FT

Bed A

1. Cucumbers then Beets
2. 20 Canning Tomatoes/Radish/ Basil
3. 20 Canning Tomatoes/Parsley/Marigold every 2 ft.
4. 20 Canning Tomates/Zinnia every 2ft.
5. 20 Slicer Tomatoes/Herb of choice
6. 20 Slicer Tomatoes/Gazinia/Marigold
7. 20 Slicer Tomatoes
8. 20 Cherry Tomatoes
9. Row 1 10 Eggplant, Row 2 Loose Leaf Lettuce
10. Three Rows Sweet Peppers-staggered (28)
11. 2 Rows Sweet Peppers–staggered (18), Row 1 Cilantro/Flowers
12. 2 Rows Sweet Peppers–staggered (18), Row 1 Raddichio/Edive (Any Green)
13. Head Lettuce (three rows (60) head). Start 20 heads week 1, 20 heads week 2, 20 heads week 3. When time to transplant you can fill the whole bed but not have 60 heads ready at the same time.
14. Leaf Lettuce- Scatter Sown.
15. Sunflowers, Edive/Arugula/Radiccio/Greens
16. Lettuce/Kale/Cucumbers on Fence

Bed B

1. (5) Winter Squash Bush variety, Marigold, Basil between Make sure they mature so they are well established buy the time the sqash sprouts.
2. Head Lettuce (three rows (60) head). Start 20 heads week 1, 20 heads week 2, 20 heads week 3. When time to transplant you can fill the whole bed but not have 60 heads ready at the same time.
3.
4. (5) Winter Squash Bush variety, Marigold, Basil between Make sure they mature so they are well established buy the time the sqash sprouts.
5. (5) Summer Squash, 3 Sunflowers between
6. Two Row Celery, 1 Row Marigold
7. 2 Row Radish/Watermellon Radish, 1 Row Zinnia, Follow Radish with Summer Squash/Zucchini
8. Row 1 Dahlia, 1 Row Swiss chard, 1 Row Curly Kale
9. Three Rows Beets, Replace Beets with 2 Row Green Beans, 1 Row Dill
10. 2 Rows Spinach, Green Beans (Replace Spinach with Sucession Sowing of Green Beans)
11. 2 Rows Leeks, 1 Row Snapdragon/Dahlia
12. Three Rows Carrots
13. Three Rows Sweet Spanish Onions
14. Three Rows Storage Onions
15. Three Rows Spring or Fall Sown
16. Shallots (Onions), Spinach and Marigolds/Flower

THE GROWER'S GARDEN 132FT X 55FT

Side A.

1. Row 1 Large Sweet onions, Row 2 & 3 Leeks,
2. Row 1, 2, 3 Carrots
3. Row 1 & 2 parsnips, sunflowers.
4. Row 1 Zinnia, Row 2 Swiss Chard, Row 3 Loose Leaf
5. Row 1 Lacinato Kale, Row 2 Swiss Chard, Row 3 Loose Leaf
6. Row 1 Head Butter Green, Row 2 Butter Red, Row 3 Head lettuce
7. Row 1 Green Bean, Row 2 Watermelon Radish/Radish, Row 3 Green Beans
8. Three Rows staggered Sweet Peppers end cap rows with cilantro and Flower of choice
9. Row 1 Sweet Pepper, Row 2 Kale, Endive, Radicchio (alternating), Marigold/Gazinia
10. Three Rows of storage onion (Red/Yellow)
11. Row 1 Head lettuce, Row 2 Snapdragon (cut flower), Row 3 Herb of choice
12. 2 Rows staggered Cherry Tomatoes (Dwarf for easy trellising), interplant basil
13. 2 Rows staggered Slicer Tomatoes (Dwarf for easy trellising), interplant basil
14. Row 1 Marrigold, Row 2 Celery, Row 3 Beets
15. 2 Rows staggered Canner Tomatoes stake for support, interplant basil
16. 2 Rows staggered Canner Tomatoes stake for support, interplant basil
17. 2 Rows staggered Canner Tomatoes stake for support, interplant basil
18. 1 Row Cucumbers on the inside of fence

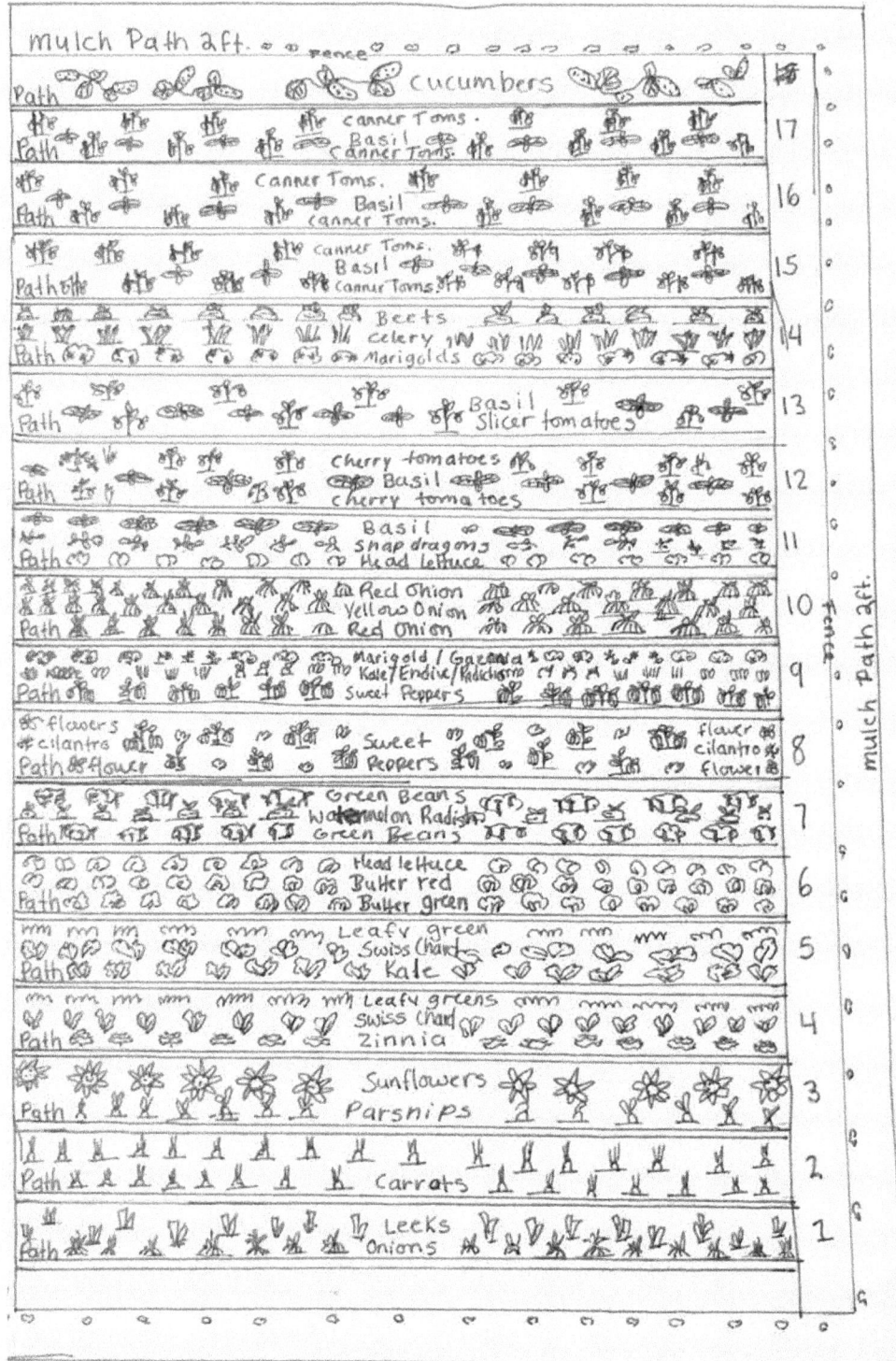

mulch Path 2ft. — fence

- Path — Cucumbers — 18
- Path — canner Toms. / Basil / canner Toms. — 17
- Path — Canner Toms. / Basil / canner Toms. — 16
- Path — canner Toms. / Basil / canner Toms. — 15
- Path — Beets / celery / Marigolds — 14
- Path — Basil / Slicer tomatoes — 13
- Path — cherry tomatoes / Basil / cherry tomatoes — 12
- Path — Basil / snapdragons / Head lettuce — 11
- Path — Red Onion / Yellow Onion / Red Onion — 10
- Path — Marigold/Gazinia / Kale/Endive/Radicchio / Sweet Peppers — 9
- Path — flowers & cilantro & flower / Sweet Peppers / flower cilantro & flower — 8
- Path — Green Beans / Watermelon Radish / Green Beans — 7
- Path — Head lettuce / Butter red / Butter green — 6
- Path — Leafy green / Swiss Chard / Kale — 5
- Path — leafy greens / Swiss chard / Zinnia — 4
- Path — Sunflowers / Parsnips — 3
- Path — Carrots — 2
- Path — Leeks / Onions — 1

mulch Path 2ft.

222

THE GROWER'S GARDEN 4500+ SQ FT

Critter Proof-Perimeter: For additional protection add a 2ft wide mulch path around the entire garden plant a 30 in pest repelling perimeter bed. One row Marigold/Perennial Herbs alternating. Fall Sown: One row Onions, One row garlic OR Spring sown: 2 rows onions

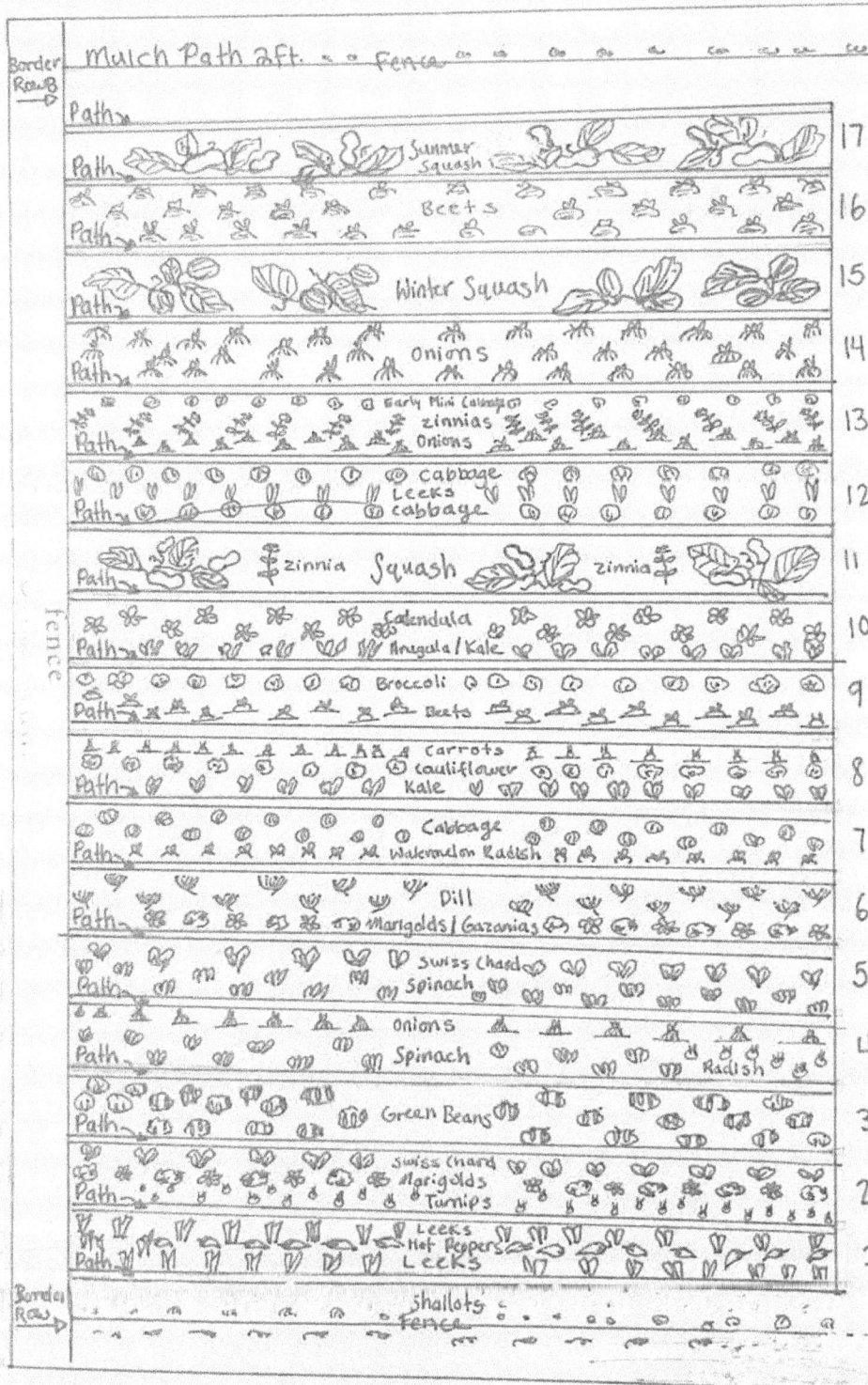

Diagram labels (left side, top to bottom):
- Border Row B →
- Mulch Path 2ft. — Fence
- Path
- Path — Summer Squash — 17
- Beets — 16
- Path — Winter Squash — 15
- Path — Onions — 14
- Path — Early Mini Cabbage / zinnias / Onions — 13
- Path — cabbage / Leeks / cabbage — 12
- Path — zinnia Squash zinnia — 11
- Path — Calendula / Arugula / Kale — 10
- Broccoli / Beets — 9
- Path — carrots / cauliflower / Kale — 8
- Path — Cabbage / Watermelon Radish — 7
- Path — Dill / Marigolds / Gazanias — 6
- Path — Swiss Chard / Spinach — 5
- Path — Onions / Spinach / Radish — 4
- Path — Green Beans — 3
- Path — Swiss Chard / Marigolds / Turnips — 2
- Path — Leeks / Hot Peppers / Leeks — 1
- Border Row → Shallots — Fence
- fence

Side B

1. Row 1 Leeks, Row 2 & 3 Hot Peppers,
2. Row 1, 2, 3 Green Beans
3. Row 1 Swiss Chard, Row 2 Marigold/Gazinia, Row 3 Radish/Turnip.
4. Row 1 & 2 Spinach, Row 3 Cippolini Onions
5. Row 1 & 2 Swiss Chard, Gazinia/Herb Alternating
6. Row 1 Dill, Row 2 Fennel, Row 3 Herb/Flower
7. Row 1 & 2 Cabbage, Row 3 Watermelon Radish/Radish
8. Three Rows staggered Cauliflower and Marigolds
9. Three Rows staggered Broccoli and Beets
10. Rows 1 Calendula, Row 2 Arugula, Kale, Endive, Radicchio—alternating
11. Row 1 Zucchini Squash, Row 2 Snapdragon/Zinnia (cut flower)
12. Three Rows Cabbage, interplant Marigold
13. Row 1 Marigold, Row 2 Mini Cabbage, Row 3 Zinnia
14. 1Row Winter Squash, interplant Marigold
15. 3 Rows Storage Onions
16. Summer Squash, Zinnia
17. 3 Rows Beets
18. Cucumbers OR Peas on Fence

FRIENDS & FOES QUICK REFERENCE

CUCUMBERS
Friends: Beans, Corn, Radishes, Nasturtiums
Foes: Potatoes, Melons, Tomatoes, Peppers

SUMMER SQUASH
Friends: Beans, Corn, Nasturtiums, Radishes
Foes: Cucumbers, Potatoes, Zucchini

MELONS
Friends: Corn, Beans, Nasturtiums, Radishes
Foes: Cucumbers, Potatoes, Carrots

WINTER SQUASH
Friends: Beans, Corn, Marigolds, Nasturtiums
Foes: Potatoes, Tomatoes, Cucumbers

ONIONS
Friends: Lettuce, Carrots, Strawberries
Foes: Beans, Peas

GARLIC
Friends: Tomatoes, Peppers, Carrots
Foes: Asparagus, Beans

LEEKS
Friends: Carrots, Celery, Onions
Foes: Beans, Peas

SHALLOTS
Friends: Carrots, Lettuce, Tomatoes
Foes: Beans, Peas

MY GARDEN

free to copy and use to plan your space

MY GARDEN

MY GARDEN

free to copy and use to plan your space

MY GARDEN

free to copy and use to plan your space

MY GARDEN

free to copy and use to plan your space

MY GARDEN

free to copy and use to plan your space

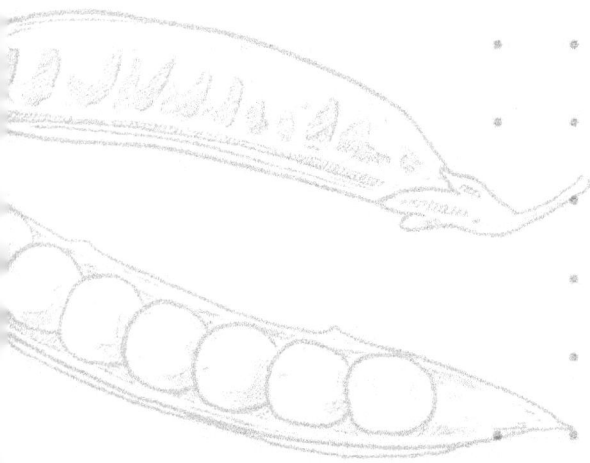

ACKNOWLEDGEMENTS

To **Valery Sykes**—thank you for your steady hand in editing this book. Your wisdom, eye for detail and kindness shaped every page.

To **Diane**—thank you for telling me not to give up when I needed to hear it most. To the countless friends who asked questions, sat through practice lessons, and cheered me on with honest curiosity and contagious excitement—you kept me going.

To **Andrea**—thank you for being our biggest fan from day one.

To my team of prayer warriors—you know who you are. Thank you. You are amazing.

Mom, thank you for making us write. Generations will never be the same. **Dad,** I miss you.

And most of all, to my children and to **Keith**—

Kids: Thank you for being such a willing and seamless team as Mama took on *yet another* part-time job. Thank you for the grace you showed through late dinners, odd dinners, the giggles at my noise-canceling headphones, and the early morning thump of the treadmill as I wrote and jogged before the sun. Thank you for believing I should write.

To **Keith**—

You and I, we're more like acorns. Not one-season veggies—delightful and gone—but steady, rooted things. Thank you for being willing to plant deep roots, grow strong branches, and launch our most beautiful garden of all.

And finally, I love You Jesus.

Thank You.

You met me in the tending soil, planting seeds, and waiting. It became a holy, dim reflection of Eden. I am forever grateful.

"…A farmer planted seed. As he scattered the seed… Some fell on good earth, and produced a harvest beyond his wildest dreams."

— *Matthew 13:7–8, MSG*

INDEX

Resources to Grow With

This is by no means a comprehensive list, just a few favorites. Here's where we turn when we're ready to dig in.

Seed Companies We Love

High Mowing Organic Seeds

Premium, certified organic seeds from growers who practice what they preach. Website: *www.highmowingseeds.com*

Botanical Interests

Beautiful packets, helpful guides, and a perfect place for beginner gardeners. Website: *www.botanicalinterests.com*

True Leaf Market

Bulk seeds, microgreens, heirlooms, and unique varieties for the curious grower. Website: *www.trueleafmarket.com*

We Carry Seeds Too!

We proudly carry High Mowing Seed for our local customers and offer exclusive discounts. Email us: DEALS jointhefamily@deeprivergardens.com for the latest deals.

Meet us at the Market!

Stop by our booth for exclusive seed deals, quick garden chats, and the community feel you've been craving. Bring your questions—and your tomato dreams.

People & Pages That Inspire

Jessica Sowards – Roots and Refuge

A beautiful, poetic soul with a deep love for tomatoes, children, and cultivating life. Her YouTube channel overflows with practical, lived wisdom, and encouragement for beginner and seasoned growers alike.

Charles Dowding – No Dig Gardening

Legendary no-dig advocate with decades of experience. His simple, soil-first method cuts the work and boosts the harvest.

Justin Rhodes – The Rooted Life

From chickens to compost, Justin shares it all—family, farm, and failures included. Entertaining, honest, and full of grit and joy. Both of you have inspired us more than you know. More than a homestead we've been able to build a healthy farm-family because of your example. That is eternal.

Shawn & Beth Dougherty – The Independent Farmstead

This book offers a real-world guide to regenerative living, particularly on the small scale. A thoughtful, practical blueprint for nourishing your household straight from the land. Your encouragement and passion came when we needed it most.

Joel Salatin – You Can Farm

Bold and unfiltered, this modern classic sparked a movement. A must-read for anyone dreaming of turning their homestead into a livelihood. No nonsense and practical, Joel will inpire and challenge you to make your passions profitable.

Ask Us Anything!

We love hearing from fellow growers, dreamers, and dirt lovers. Comments, DM's, or carrier pigeons.

Facebook: @deeprivergardens Instagram: @15mingardener
Web: www.deeprivergardens.com
Email: jointhefamily@deeprivergardens.com

SOURCES

Bradley, Fern Marshall. *The Organic Gardener's Handbook of Natural Pest and Disease Control*. Rodale Books, 2009.

Burke, Nicole. *The Kitchen Garden Revival: A Modern Guide to Creating a Stylish, Small-Scale, Low-Maintenance, Edible Garden*. Ten Speed Press, 2020.

Coleman, Eliot. *The Winter Harvest Handbook: Year-Round Vegetable Production Using Deep-Organic Techniques and Unheated Greenhouses*. Chelsea Green Publishing, 2012.

Coleman, Eliot. *The New Organic Grower*. Chelsea Green Publishing, 1995. Dowding,
Charles. *No Dig Organic Home & Garden*. Green Books, 2017.
Gilbertie, Sal, and Larry Sheehan. *Small-Plot, High-Yield Gardening: Grow Like a Pro, Save Money, and Eat Well from Your Front (or Back Side) Yard 100% Organic Produce Garden*. Ten Speed Press, 1999.

Richardson, Joan. *Wild Edible Plants of New England*. 1st ed., 2018.

Sowards, Jessica. *Roots and Refuge: A Modern Homesteader's Guide to Growing, Gardening, and Dreaming Big*. Harvest House Publishers, 2021.

About the Author

Lisa Douglass is a farmer, homeschooling mother, and lifelong student of the soil, living and growing in the challenging climate of upstate New York. On a rugged 55-acre property, she and her husband are raising their eleven children—ten still at home—amid a landscape that demands resilience and rewards those who pay attention. Lisa's days are spent tending not only to vegetables and livestock, but also to the rhythms of family life and education, where learning is shaped by both books and the seasons.

Her approach to gardening is practical, rooted in observation and the lived experience of cultivating food through snow, thaw, and short growing windows. She is particularly drawn to the deeper questions of sustainability, local resilience, and the role of family in stewarding land. What started as a personal effort to feed her household has grown into a wider mission: to encourage others to grow what they can, where they are, and to reimagine the possibilities of homegrown food—even in hard conditions.

Through writing and mentoring, Lisa shares the lessons she's learned from failures, frost dates, and the quiet power of persistence. She's not offering a fantasy of farm life, but a working model—messy, grounded, and real—for how cultivating a small piece of earth can shape both a home and a community.

About the Artists

A few of the illustrations in this book hold extra meaning—they were created by the author's daughter, Sadie Douglass, a talented young artist whose eye for detail has earned her top honors at the New York State Fair. Sadie brought the garden scenes to life with warmth and precision, building on the original sketches done by her sister Keira Douglass, who helped conceptualize the designs from the ground up. Together, they form a remarkable creative team—both dedicated growers who understand the rhythms of the garden as deeply as they do the nuances of pencil and paper. Their work is more than artistic contribution; it's an extension of the family's shared commitment to growing, learning, and creating side by side.

www.ingramcontent.com/pod-product-compliance
Lightning Source LLC
Chambersburg PA
CBHW041611260326
41914CB00012B/1456